The Face of Social Suffering

The Life History of a Street Drug Addict

MERRILL SINGER

University of Connecticut

WAVELAND

PRESS, INC.

Long Grove, Illinois

To Pam

For information about this book, contact:
 Waveland Press, Inc.
 4180 IL Route 83, Suite 101
 Long Grove, IL 60047-9580
 (847) 634-0081
 info@waveland.com
 www.waveland.com

Cover art: Painting by Jacob Singer
All text photographs by Merrill Singer

Copyright © 2006 by Waveland Press, Inc.

10-digit ISBN 1-57766-432-9
13-digit ISBN 978-1-57766-432-1

Printed in the United States of America

8   7   6   5   4   3

Contents

iii

Preface

I began studying the abuse, initially of legal and later of illegal drugs, in 1979 at the Institute for Family Research at George Washington University in Washington, D.C. Before then, I had not given much thought to psychotropic drugs as a research topic; since then, by contrast, it has been central to my life as a medical anthropologist with a commitment to addressing community-based health and health disparity issues. Much of this time, I have worked at the Hispanic Health Council in Hartford, CT, including during the research projects that gave rise to this book.

Over the course of the last twenty-five years, I have had the opportunity to interview many drug users and have been a part of research initiatives that have included over 5,000 drug users in one-on-one interviews about their experiences with drugs and the health and social consequences of use. Sometimes this has involved basic research, other times applied research designed to test the efficacy of intervention models to prevent disease, lower drug use, or assist participants to enter drug treatment.

During the course of this work, in 1998, I met the individual whose life is detailed in the pages that follow. Like the Puerto Rican agricultural worker who's life history was told by Sidney Mintz, he is "neither a public figure nor a famous man, nor prestigious nor distinguished" (1974:ix). I call him Tony here, but that is not his real name. It is fitting that his identity should be hidden behind a pseudonym, because like most street drug users, for most of society he is more or less invisible. If, as Henry David Thoreau proposed, the mass of men lead lives of quiet desperation, Tony's life, over time, has been not only quietly desperate but generally pushed to the margins, to places where desperation is intended to be quiet, nondisturbing, and unimportant. We can all feel okay about Tony's problems because, after all, they are "Tony's problems," not ours. They are, as we like to believe, of his own making. No one forces him to remain a drug addict, to participate in criminal acts, to be violent, to do the kinds of things that have led to his repeated incarceration and to infection with HIV and hepatitis. "He has no one to blame but himself" goes the mantra of American individual responsibility and privatized suffering. This way of thinking about the issue has a natural authenticity to it: it is simple, straightforward, and appears to follow from our personal everyday experiences as decision makers. We see that we make choices—should I turn left or right—and those choices have consequences. When we make bad decisions, we know—as we like to phrase it given our cultural penchant for militaristic imagery—"no one had a gun to our head."

But what if, even for only a fleeting moment, we suspend our culturally constituted denial of social responsibility, if only to answer the questions: do we want ours to be the kind of society where everyone matters, even if they are not the same color as almost every single Senator who now holds office and draws a considerable paycheck of taxpayer dollars? Do we want a society where we do not send people who break the law to training institutes for enhanced criminality (known colloquially as prisons) where they can learn their craft from the masters, but instead we address their issues and needs so that when they return to live among us—and the vast majority of cons become ex-cons—they pray with us rather than prey upon us? Can we envision a society in which the poor are not forced to self-medicate the hidden injuries of daily oppression by using illicit and often quite harmful drugs purchased on the street in contexts of threat and violence, drugs that make some people very addicted and others very rich (not just bad men in distant lands who speak foreign languages, but the English-speaking White Anglo-Saxon shareholders of the wealthiest pharmaceutical companies who make more and more of the magical chemicals used by illicit drug users, and the enormously wealthy doctors who prescribe pain-deadening pills left and right as if they did not know most get diverted into illicit use, and the presidents of Fortune 500 banks that quietly launder drug profits with a wink and a blind eye to the source of their reinvestable deposits, and so on and on and on)? Is it possible for ours to be a society in which the real pain of social inequality is taken seriously as a call to social action rather than as useful source material for celluloid fantasies and movie company profit?

Since that is the type of world I want my children to live in, by trying to make one hidden life more visible, this book seeks to contribute to the building of such a society. Its goal, in other words, is to put a human face on someone whose plight is easily dismissed because of his lifetime of "bad choices." Further, it seeks to unveil the ways in which this individual's behavior is far from uniquely his, far from solely a product of his personal decisions and actions, but instead submerged within a strongly influencing context of structurally imposed social suffering. Social suffering (Kleinman, Das, and Lock 1997) refers to the immediate personal experience of broad human problems caused by the exercise of political and economic power, such as war, oppression, torture, and poverty. In other words, social suffering refers to what power does to people, people like Tony. As Rebecca Chopp comments:

> Knowledge of suffering cannot be conveyed in pure facts and figures, reportings that objectify the suffering of countless persons. The horror of suffering is not only in its immensity but in the faces of the anonymous victims who have little voice, let alone rights, in history. (1986:2)

This book, in short, is about going beyond the facts and figures, useful as they are, to find the face of social suffering. By peeking through the pane of suffering in the life of one individual, it seeks to pierce "the encrustations of bureaucratic and theoretical talk that have muffled the voice of individuals in pain" (Schwarcz 1997:120).

ACKNOWLEDGMENTS

This book is dedicated to Pam, because she endured its unfolding, hour after hour, day after day, with grace, tolerance, loving support, and readily available editorial assistance and advice. Writing a book sometimes is a very lonely experience, and then, sometimes not. This time, happily, it wasn't. Of course, this book would not have been possible without "Tony," as this is about his life as best as he or I could understand it. As always, I am indebted to my colleagues at the Hispanic Health Council, especially Jeannette DeJesus, the executive director, who understands that writing late into the night makes for sleepy mornings; Lucy Rohena, who helped keep me in touch with Tony over the years; Erica Hastings, who helped with transcription; Joan Cruz, for making sure that I pulled myself away from the computer to get to meetings on time; and Greg Mirhej, for minding the store and lending an ear, and getting all the jokes. Once again, my editors at Waveland, Tom Curtin and Jeni Ogilvie, have my warmest thanks. Lastly, I would like to express gratitude to Eric Wolf, whose work long has been and remains an inspiration. I was finally able to tell him this prior to his untimely death; of his many students who rose to acknowledge his beneficial influence, I was the single one who had never actually taken one of his courses.

• Chapter 1 •

A Life
on the Edge

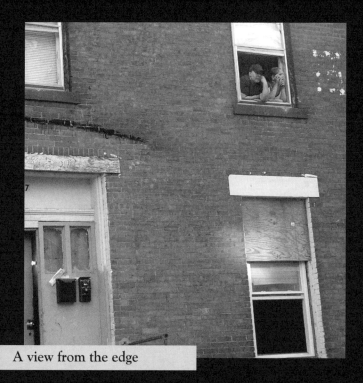

A view from the edge

[S]o many people in our society . . . live their lives without fulfilling their personal goals. Yet, though they may die without realizing their human potential, they die fighting. At the same time their voices are so muted by their unyielding circumstances that many of us are rarely compelled, even for one moment, to reflect upon their toll. Yet, these human beings are not so defeated as it might seem; for the most part they make do with what they have and at times manifest a nobility and courage that is astonishing.

—Felix Padilla and Lourdes Santiago, Outside the Wall

If we continue to make poverty and lifestyle the basis for justice and punishment, then the urban crisis will continue.

—James Spradley, You Owe Yourself a Drunk

INTO A LIFE

I am sitting across from Tony on a makeshift chair in a dimly lit, partially demolished abandoned building in the heart of the inner city of Hartford. Deserted buildings like this one, that once were warm, lighted, and filled with the daily lives and activities of local residents, dot the urban landscape—reminders of the wasteful consumer-oriented use and discard lifestyles we have come to lead. The walls around us are covered with hastily applied graffiti, an ever-present commentary in a world of anonymous public authors. They appear as brief testament to silent voices that demand to be heard. The ruins of buildings like this one do not last long, however. Within a year of the day Tony and I sat there, with me firing questions and him responding, the building had been turned to rubble and carted away. Today it is a vacant lot, part of the missing-tooth look that has replaced the smile of urban life.

On the day that Tony and I met up there to conduct an interview, as I looked around the room, the floor suggested a recent hurricane, but in fact exemplified the common chaotic décor of the structures we build and leave behind as we abandon the older inner cores of our cities for greener pastures that lie further from those places we glibly call "bad areas"; in the process, of course, we label those who still live in the city center—the poor, the socially unacceptable, and often people of color—as dangerous, diseased, and immoral. Scattered about is a very mixed array of trash, abandoned clothing, scraps of newspapers that probably went unread, an occasional torn page of pornography, human excrement, discarded water bottles, AIDS prevention pamphlets, and an occasional syringe left behind by the steady traffic of street drug users who slip in for a brief moment of privacy and protection from the threatening gaze of the police while they inject drugs into their battered bodies. As he usually does at this time of day, Tony

3

is in the process of "fixing," the street name for preparing his next injection of illicit heroin, which he purchased just minutes earlier from a young street drug dealer. The exchange was quick and obscure, but for Tony, an addict, it was vital. In the process, $9 or $10 more slipped down the ravenous funnel of the illicit drug trade, and Tony procured the small bag of innocent looking white powder that had probably traveled thousands of miles, across the borders of numerous countries, past the watchful eyes of countless soldiers in the grim War on Drugs, to find its way into his vein.

I am looking across at Tony; he is soft-spoken, almost deferential. But I know his outer calm is a mask, a face he turns to the world to disguise the intense inner conflict that makes him forever restless and moody. He often is frustrated and in a state of turmoil because of his uncertainty about how to extricate himself from a constant barrage of economic, interpersonal, and health problems. He finds some peace, briefly and at grave cost, in illicit drugs. They bring him the few peaceful moments he knows in days and nights spent "ripping and running" and barely coping.

Before him, set on an old box, are Tony's "works," including the bottle top he will use to mix the powdered drug with water from a small plastic bottle, a small piece of cotton that he will employ as a filter so that any undissolved powder does not clog up and ruin his needle, his plastic insulin syringe, and, on this day at least, an alcohol swab to clean the injection site on his arm before injecting the drug directly into his vein, a process known on the street as mainlining. As he repeats a ritual he has performed hundreds if not thousands of times since he was a teenager, Tony quickly answers my cascade of questions about each step in the injection process.

He endures my questions, endless though they may seem, because we have been working together for years now (7 years at the time of this writing), whenever he is back out on the street from his latest stint in jail for a drug-related or other crime. He knows that I can be counted on as a source of money to pay for his time during each interview. In turn, in light of the intimate details of his life and the suffering that he has shared, the consistency of his comments over time, and verification from interviews conducted with many other street drug users, I have grown confident that within reason he tries to tell the truth about his drug use behaviors, his life, and his hopes about somehow, some day turning his life around into something better, something more respectable than spending his days shooting up illegal drugs in a godforsaken wreckage of a building.

KNOWING OTHER LIVES

This book is written as a life history of Tony (a pseudonym, as are the names of people and places used in the book that might expose Tony's identity), a lifelong drug dealer and drug addict of mixed Italian and Irish heritage. The book is intended to sympathetically tell the fast-paced, darkly adventurous, and often disturbing story of Tony's life growing up in the inner city, becoming drug addicted, peddling drugs to others, going to jail, serving frequently as an enforcer of the heartless rules in a youth street gang—which at times was a gruesomely violent role—and living out his life in the menacing shadows on the margins of conventional society. Hard-core, drug-involved individuals like Tony are often presented as public enemies, the people who break into our homes, steal our possessions, mug us on city streets, make our cities unlivable, lure our children into wasted lives, spread disease, and, more recently, through their drug purchases, support international terrorism. Against these jagged images of danger and destruction, Tony is presented here much as he presents himself to the world, a tall but unassertive man who lives his life on the biting edge of crisis, a crisis that, while reflecting his own choices and actions, is nonetheless far beyond his capacity to control.

Herein lies an important reason Tony's life history merits telling. He inhabits the same world we do, yet his is a denizen of regions rarely if ever visited by most of us. Moreover, his immediate day-to-day world and the larger social world around him are not really two separate domains. They intertwine, endlessly producing consequences both for people like Tony and for the rest of society as well. As I have argued elsewhere (Singer 2006:156):

> From the laundering of drug profits by mainstream banking
> institutions to the shopkeeper purchase "on the cheap" of
> items shoplifted by drug addicts from competitors as a way to
> cut overhead, and from heroin chic designer clothes displayed
> on fashion runways in Paris to the reinvestment of drug profits
> in legal business, the aboveground mainstream economy and
> the belowground drug economy are, in the end, one economy
> that consists of two closely intertwined components.

This book is intended as a window on the shadowy, hidden side of
modern urban life.

As expressed by sociologist C. Wright Mills in his seminal
book *The Sociological Imagination* (1959:1), "Neither the life of an
individual nor the history of a society can be understood without
understanding both." Indeed, French sociologist Pierre Bourdieu
(1990:67) has complained of "the absurd opposition between individual and society" commonly found in public discourse and social
commentary. In other words, examining the ups and downs and
other intricacies of a life, any life, without locating that life in history, in society, and in an array of particular social locations within
that society, such as social class, geographic region, ethnicity, and
gender, would be folly. We do not come into the world and make
ourselves *sui generis* (i.e., out of nothing). Rather we significantly
are influenced and shaped, in our values, our understandings, and
our experiences, by our social locations and cultural milieux.

At the same time, as Anthony Wallace points out, "One of the
most hoary assumptions" made about culture and personality "is the
belief that a society will fall apart and its members scatter if they are
not threaded like beads on a string of common motives" (1970:24).
In any society, in fact, there is a diversity of personalities, motives,
and attitudes, held together, more or less, by cultural systems, ritualized events, and institutions for organizing diversity. Moreover, the
social locations we inhabit change, in part because we change them.
As individuals, we are active, decision-making agents who are capable of not always doing what was done before or what is expected of
us by others. We innovate, we adjust, we test new possibilities. At
the social level, rather than being fixed and frozen, groups tend to
"exploit the ambiguities of inherited [cultural] forms, to impart new

evaluations or valences to them, to borrow forms more expressive of their interests, or to create wholly new forms to answer changed circumstance" (Wolf 1982:387). Truly, we make new social worlds, but hardly just as we would like them to be.

Examining an individual life, thus serves as one means of bridging what might be termed the "micro-macro dilemma" in contemporary social science (Singer 1997). As DeWalt and Pelto observe, "articulating the linkages between microlevels and macrolevels" in society has become "among the most vexing issues in social science research" while at the same time emerging as "a most promising area for current research and theory building" (1985:4). Addressing this dilemma through life histories provides one means of repersonalizing both the subject matter of social science as well as taken-for-granted beliefs in public discourse (e.g., assumptions about street drug dealers). This is achieved by focusing attention on "the particular, the existential, the subjective content of . . . suffering" (Scheper-Hughes and Lock 1986:137) as both actual event and lived experience, while avoiding the tendency in our society to overlook the degree to which we do not live in natural worlds but in socially constructed ones.

THE HISTORY OF LIFE HISTORY

Life histories of what some would call deviant lives, individuals Dan Waldorf (1973) colorfully called the "people of the other side, those outside the pale, [in] what used to be known as the low life [and would today be called 'on the down-low']" have a social history of their own. Consisting of both biographies and autobiographies, this gritty genre has been used to poignantly convey to interested outsiders the inner experiential worlds of individuals from hidden populations not readily accessible to less dramatic forms of social research. Unlike portrayals based on surveys of a population or interviews with multiple members of a group, the life history charts a single life as a microcosm of, at least to some degree, a wider group of people that are little known, perhaps gravely misunderstood, and often maligned.

Life histories of this sort are not written of famous people; on the contrary, they describe the lives of the obscure, the downtrodden, and the silenced (Mintz 1974). In this, they help to complete the story of our world, a world that would otherwise appear to be inhabited only by kings and presidents, generals and the rich. Further, as Michael McCall and Judith Wittner maintain:

> Because they depend less on concepts grounded in the experiences of social dominant groups and classes, life histories deepen the critique of existing knowledge. They force us to examine our assumptions, incorporate more actors into our models, and generate more inclusive concepts for understanding the actual complexities of social institutions and the processes of social change. (1990:46)

Most importantly, because they can bring us into intimate awareness of lives lived under very different and often much more difficult circumstances than our own, life histories can remind us of our responsibility to help move "towards a social structure in which there is less exploitation, oppression, and injustice and more creativity, diversity and equality" (McCall and Wittner 1990:52).

On the autobiographic side of the life history genre, Thomas De Quincey's (1822) *Confessions of an English Opium Eater* is without doubt the oldest example of narrative encounter with the nether world of socially marginal behavior, especially of mind-altering drug use. By "tearing away that 'decent drapery'" that shields proper society from the darker regions of human activity, De Quincey (1822:xxiii), like all writers in this mode, sought to elucidate the core by exploring its margins. William Bourroughs' (1953) *Junkie*, Piri Thomas' (1967) *Down These Mean Streets*, and Art Pepper's (1999) *Straight Life* are considered classic biographies of turbulent, often pain-filled yet unflinching drug-involved lives. "Cupid's Story," an autobiographical account of a gang member, appears as a chapter in R. Lincoln Keiser's (1969) ethnographic account *The Vice Lords: Warriors of the Street*. Like Tony, Cupid was a fighter for whom intense violence was normal and expected. Not all life histories are of men, of course, and Felix Padilla and Lourdes Santiago's (1993) *Outside the Wall* provides a woman's perspective on the drug scene that swallowed up her friends and family members. On the biographical side of the aisle, Clifford Shaw's (1976) *The Natural History of a Delinquent Career* and Edwin Sutherland's (1937) *Professional Thief* added very early insight into the nature and meaning of deviant careers. Rettig's (1977) *Manny: A Criminal-Addict's Story* mixed biography and social science investigation to tell the tale of "deviance, crime, correction, and criminal justice" from the viewpoint of one man caught up in a drug-fueled drive to "anesthetize . . . the whole damn ugly world" (13). Other important works in this bibliography include Eldrige Cleaver's (1968) *Soul On Ice*, Bill Sands' (1964) *My Shadow Ran Fast*, Malcolm X's (1965) *The Autobiography of Malcolm X*, and Theodore Rubin's (1961) *In the Life*. In *A Rainbow of Gangs: Street Cultures in the Mega-City* (2002), longtime drug researcher, James Diego Vigil provides comparable accounts of the life histories of individuals from Mexican American, African American, Vietnamese, and Salvadoran gangs in Los Angeles, revealing therein that individual lives reflect far broader social and cultural patterns and that diverse groups subject to similar social conditions can produce individuals with much in common.

As a medical anthropologist, who for the last 25 years has been regularly involved in the study of drinking and illicit drug use and its public health impact (Singer 2006), I have tapped many resources to gain insights, and the existing array of drug-user narratives have been crucial in building my understanding of the behaviors, attitudes, experiences, and contexts of psychotropic consumption through time. While like these other books in some ways, this book is unique in its public health orientation. It asks the question: what does a life like Tony's tell us about how to address the health threats of drugs, including a range of old and new drug-mediated diseases spreading in society, in ways that are effective, efficient and culturally and socially appropriate? Adding this book to the existing body of work is intended to enrich our comprehension of the continued appeal of drugs even at a time when essentially all drug users know about drug use's connection to deadly and damaging diseases like HIV, hepatitis, tuberculosis, botulism, and sexually transmitted infections.

From a public health standpoint, as the AIDS epidemic has made clear, drug users are biologically part of society, ultimately inseparable from the rest of us even with the use of late night police raids and expensive prison cells. Knowing their world better, its many twists and rapid turns, and the forces that contribute to frequent risky behaviors is imperative in the midst of spreading global epidemic (an epidemic, ironically, during which injection drug use has been spreading to new populations who are quickly put at risk for HIV and other infections).

Additionally, Tony's story is worth telling because drugs often influence what happens and why it happens in our society and in the wider world in ways that we little realize and might not readily acknowledge if we did. While drug users are often marginalized and written out of history, they and the drugs they use can influence the course of events. The war in Vietnam is a case in point. Certainly a factor in the U.S. decision to pull out of that war and bring our weary troops home was the fact that drug addiction had sapped the capacity of many units to continue to engage in battle. Similarly, little recognized is the fact that the search for psychotropic drugs was part of the reason the Spanish throne financed Columbus to sale westward resulting in his unexpected "discovery" of a New World, and that drugs like tobacco, which Columbus brought back with him to Europe, helped to pay for the industrial revolution while helping to maintain and control the working class as they were converted from peasant farmers into "wage slaves." Even Hitler's fall may well have been influenced by the powerful psychotropic drugs (i.e., amphetamines) being administered to him daily by his personal physician. Moreover, our country and many others besides have been engaged in a massively expensive War on Drugs for several generations, and yet people like Tony continue to readily find illicit drugs at relatively cheap prices on street corners throughout the inner city. Here, too, his story holds lessons about issues of wider magnitude and public concern.

Finally, Tony's story is of interest for the role it serves as a sometimes unkind mirror on our society and how we handle and often mishandle diversity and cultural difference. How we socially construct drug users—and use these constructed images to guide our treatment of them—is revealing of the kind of society we inhabit. Drug users have been called the modern bogeymen, scapegoats for evils whose true source remains hidden from everyday view. Put otherwise, there is much to learn about the top of society in all of its hidden and exposed complexity by studying how those at the bottom are depicted. For these reasons studying the lives of drug users like Tony remains a fundamental task within the social sciences.

If nothing else this book seeks to present Tony as I have come to know him—a man like myself with heartfelt hopes and fears, struggling to make it in a world that is often harsh, regularly indifferent, and at times life threatening. If Tony as a living, breathing, thinking, and hurting person were kept in mind in every policy discussion about what to do about the "drug problem," I suspect that we would come up with far better "solutions" than those that guide contemporary actions from the failed War on Drugs to the far less than adequate (and far less than systematic) drug treatment "system."

THE THEORETICAL ORIENTATION OF THE BOOK

In its approach to drug use, this book follows the anthropological impulse to discover the insider's point of view. As most anthropologists see it, the process of making sense of the behavior of others, especially behavior like illicit drug use that is abhorred and condemned by mainstream institutions, best begins with learning the point of view of the enactors of the behaviors in question. Following in the tradition of James Spradley's (1970:6) *You Owe Yourself a Drunk*, "this book is an attempt to build a bridge of understanding" by providing a close-up glimpse of the life of one drug user, unique in its detail but paralleling in fundamental ways the lives of many drug users on the streets of America's tarnished cities.

Moreover, the approach taken in the interpretations presented of Tony's life in social and historic context is guided by the

theoretical orientation known as critical medical anthropology
(CMA). This orientation, which developed during the 1980s
among medical anthropologists, is concerned with locating
health-risk and other health-related behaviors, illness and disease, and medical treatment systems as well, within an encom-
passing political-economic framework of causes and determinants
of human decision making and action. From the critical perspective, explanations that seek to account for health-related issues
and behaviors only in terms of the influence of human personalities, culturally constituted motivations and understandings, or
local ecological relationships are inadequate because this blurs
the impact of *structures of social relationship*, including unequal and
oppressive social connections like interclass relations, on human
action. Critical medical anthropology, by contrast, pays close
attention to the effects of the vertical links connecting the social
group under study (in this case street drug users) to larger
regional, national, and global social units.

From the CMA perspective, drug abuse, is not so much an
expression of moral or legal failing, as it is an unhealthy selection
of a chemical solution to discomforting experiences—whether
such experiences be the misery of domestic violence, the pain
born from the assault on one's dignity caused by prolonged unemployment, the internalized rage of injustice and racial discrimination, or the bland boredom of teen life in suburbia. In Tony's case,
drugs were clearly a form of self-medication for a range of emotional problems that ultimately were rooted in the reigning structures of social inequality, as detailed in the following pages.

The selection of this response appears to have been shaped by
two factors: the cultural context that constructed self-medication
as a sanctioned coping mechanism for meeting life's demands
(Vuckovic 1999) and, because of structural factors, the ready
availability and popularity in the inner city of psychotropic drugs
capable of achieving this end. As Stuart Hills observers, in our
society "drugs obtained from the pharmacist hold out the promise
of instant relief for psychological pains" (1980:129). The generali-
zation of this pattern (which involves both the addition of illicitly
produced drugs like heroin and the diversion of pharmaceutical

drugs like Xanax to street use) flows easily from the basic cultural practice of self-medicating distress.

Unfortunately, there has been somewhat of a misunderstanding among some medical anthropologists about the orientation of CMA in accounting for the actions and experiences of people who suffer illness, including drug addiction. Janice Harper, while generally embracing a CMA perspective, faults this orientation for taking a "top-down approach . . . in which political and economic forces press down upon people represented as having relatively little autonomy or power" over their health, illness, or lives (2002:178). Others complain that "'Critical' medical anthropologists tend to see all experiences of body/self disorder as a potential register for social critique and resistance" (Brodwin (1996:197). In fact, in several prior life history and narrative accounts of people like Tony—in that they too are chemically dependent, suffering from HIV, and/or struggling at the lower rungs of the steep social ladder that defines access to resources in our society (Mosack et al. 2005, Singer et al. 1992, Singer et al. 2001, Singer and Garcia 1989)—critical medical anthropologists have shown that however much political and economic structures do in fact press down on people, people are not programmed automatons or mindless reactors to imposed constraint. They resist social forces, in ways big and small, sweeping and obscure. Sometimes they even rebel and overthrow social systems and those who had previously been in positions of greatest power. Short of this, they do many things, including, like Tony, not playing by conventional rules and regulations. As a result—also like Tony—they sometimes get arrested, beaten, up, and incarcerated. But even behind prison walls, people carve out their own lives, often resisting the imposed authority of prison officials and guards.

At the same time, everything that people do in the face of social dominance is not resistance. People unavoidably participate in their own oppression and serve as instruments for the oppression of others. On the street, for example, people avoid arrest by informing on the crimes of others. In short, the CMA perspective seeks to understand social life and experience as a conflicted relationship between those who at any point in time have amassed a disproportionate share of power and those who must endure a disproportionate share of suffering. This is the approach taken here with reference to Tony, his life, his experiences, and his actions.

HOOKING UP WITH TONY

I first met Tony when he volunteered for a Hispanic Health Council AIDS prevention study funded by the National Institute on Drug Abuse (NIDA) that was targeted to injection drug users. Beginning with the rise of the AIDS epidemic, the Hispanic Health Council—which incredibly was first housed in the building—later abandoned and now gone—in which I interviewed Tony as he shot up heroin, has made street drug use and its health sequelae an organizational priority. While all of the participants in the NIDA study took part in a structured epidemiological interview that examined their involvement in AIDS risk behaviors, a subsample of individuals was invited to come back for a more in-depth interview about their involvement with drugs, AIDS risk, and violence. My first encounter with Tony was during this qualitative interview. I found him to be open, talkative, and likeable, and I asked him to come back for a follow-up interview to further explore his life as a drug user. Thus began an ongoing relationship with Tony that has extended long after the original study ended.

This book is based on repeated tape-recorded or, on two occasions, videotaped interviews conducted with Tony from 1998 until 2005. Most of the interviews took place at the Hispanic Health Council, in inner-city Hartford, CT, where I serve as the Director of Research. One took place, as noted, in an abandoned building as Tony injected heroin. The interviews were casual and used open-ended questions designed to promote protracted answers. While Tony talked freely, he needed multiple probes to move through any particular account of an event in his life. In and out of prison, harassed regularly by police on the street, a frequent defendant in criminal trials, he had learned to be brief and to not give up too much information. And yet, he wanted his story told, hoping, it seemed, that finally something useful might come of his life.

As I was writing this chapter, I was troubled that once again, as has often been the case during the time I have known him, Tony was out of contact. Had he died of a drug overdose? Was he hospitalized because of the deadly Human Immunodeficiency Virus that surges through his blood system? Was he beaten senseless by a drug dealer's hit man because that he failed to pay for drugs taken on consignment? Or was he back in jail, a place he knows well and may prefer to the demands and threats of living on the street? I have asked myself these questions before; I will probably ask them again in the future. Uncertainty, a growing feature of our modern world, is the norm in the life of a street drug user. Fortunately, none of the above proved to be the case, as he "showed up" again as the book was being finished, ready for another interview.

ORGANIZATION OF THE BOOK

In the chapters that follow, I will explore Tony's life up to the present. Following Padilla and Santiago (1993) and Mintz (1974) before them, I organize and present information about Tony based on the intersection of two factors: themes and chronology. Each chapter is organized by a theme or stage of his life, and the chapters are ordered in terms of the chain of events that comprise Tony's ongoing story. Themes, of course, cannot always be neatly fit into time segments or life phases. For Tony, issues like drug use or imprisonment cross over several periods of his life. Accommodating this fact has resulted in telling about some things out of chronological order because they are expressions of dominant aspects of Tony's life.

Also, like Padilla and Santiago (1993:15), because the transcriptions of multiple interviews over the course of time "produced a raw and fragmented text," as well as one in which the same issues are addressed across several sittings (guided by the fact that with each interview I knew more and could ask more precise questions or ask for amplification of issues only alluded to previously), I have made "certain basic editorial and grammatical corrections to make it more readable." Always, however, I have attempted to be true to what Tony actually said. To insure that all of his meanings are clear, I have inserted clarifications in brackets in the quotes taken from the transcribed interviews, while interspersing, in the main body of the text, commentary on broader issues, exploration of key topics, as well as presentation of findings on various studies of drug users that are pertinent to Tony's tale.

In the next chapter, "Into the World: Of Drugs and Families," I look at Tony in the context of his family of origin. At a time when family values are a topic of everyday public discussion, this chapter examines Tony's mixed-heritage family. Presented are Tony's painful views of his troubled relationship with his harsh, drug-dealing, Mafia-involved father and his emotionally supportive, if beleaguered, mother. Tony's troubled relationship with his father is shown to have a defining impact on his life course; his relationship with his mother, in turn, emerges as it does for many street drug users and street alcoholics (Singer 1985) as a well-worn tether to social stability and mainstream life. Beyond these jagged bonds, Tony's wider kin network is explored to illuminate the lives and struggles of the inner-city poor.

In chapter 3, I examine Tony's early life as a street kid. As a boy of 10, Tony went on the prowl with friends, mugging, stealing, and raising hell in the streets of Philadelphia, hidden in the shadows of Temple University (whose students provided a vulnerable set of victims for Tony's preteen street gang). This chapter tells the tale of a young life caught up in the social divisions that allow some members of society to be untroubled by the huge number of inner-city males who wind up in the criminal justice system, and others to feel that a life of crime is justifiable or at least unavoidable. Setting the stage for a future life of crime, the chapter explores Tony's early friendships and antisocial actions.

The following chapter focuses on Tony's entrée into the murky and often treacherous world of illicit drug dealing. The dope dealer is heavily demonized in contemporary society, held responsible for society's loss of a communal foundation, and arrested with impunity. Tony was thrust into the life of a dope dealer at a very early age, leading quickly to his involvement in the death of a man and to his first experience of prison life. The chapter examines Tony's exploits as a drug dealer within a context of a critical social perspective on his outlaw career.

Chapter 5 focuses on Tony's entry into street and prison gang-life. Tony has lived his life as much in as out of prison; indeed, since he was 15, he has been behind bars or in some kind of criminal justice facility more than he has been a free man. During his second incarceration, he joined a street gang, which had fundamental consequences for his subsequent life choices. Tony's numerous encounters with arrest, conviction, and jail time stem from his involvement with gangs and their illicit activities. Once in prison, Tony found, ironically, that the thick barriers meant to keep criminals out of society cannot keep society, including its illicit drugs or gangs, out of prison. On the street, he continued his ganglife enmeshed in a closed circle of intimate compatriots, fellow gang members, gangbangers, and collaborators in illicit activities.

The next chapter continues the exploration of Tony's involvement with gangs, but with a focus on his personal downward spiral and decision to seek a "walk out," that is, permission to retire as an active gang member, and instead serve only in a consulting capacity in the status of "Old Gangster." Until his mid-30s, Tony maintained his gang ties and gang ways, but ultimately the toll, emotional and physical, overwhelmed him. This chapter traces his transition to his retirement from ganglife and the reasons for this change in at least one aspect of his life story.

Chapter 7 locates Tony's life in the time of AIDS. The chapter focuses on the close entwinement of drugs, sex, and health. It examines Tony's sexual and romantic life over the years as well as his attitude about his infection with both HIV and hepatitis, his fears and struggles with other health and emotional issues, and his continued decision to keep "shooting up" heroin at every opportunity. The chapter addresses the critical question of why injection drug use continues to spread in a world of deadly syringe-mediated diseases.

The final chapter provides social science and medical anthropological reflection on Tony's life, his involvement with illicit drugs, the health issues he battles, and society's approach to illicit drug use. The chapter concludes with a review of the theoretical and practical lessons learned from examining Tony's life as an outlaw in American society. How are we to deal with people like Tony? His life story, I believe, holds the answer.

· Chapter 2 ·

Into the World
Of Drugs and Families

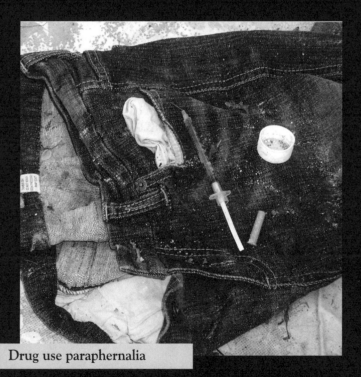

Drug use paraphernalia

*Because the community has so many problems,
over the years researchers have been tempted to search for
the roots of gang involvement in some special
characteristics of the members' families. After all,
something must make these particular young people
susceptible to the attractions of this most rowdy of youth
groups. Where better to search than the family.*

—Joan Moore, Going Down to the Barrio

*Children of the drug world experience an upbringing that
was very different from children of the larger society. . . .
In divorced households they were often bounced
back and forth from one parent to the other as the adults
fluctuated in their financial and household stability. . . .
The result of this treatment was generally a premature
precocity and independence on the children's part. . . .
[T]hese children grew up in their parents' image.*

—Patricia Adler, Wheeling and Dealing

BLOODLINES

Even street drug users have families and, often, though not always, people who love them, who suffer with them through their compelling addiction to illicit substances, who hope and pray for their recovery. Sometimes, however, family members themselves are addicts as well, fellow sojourners through the painful depths that dependency on an illicit chemical can lead. In fact, family members can be the first to introduce a person to mind altering drugs, or particular ways of using them, most commonly, as Hunt and Chambers (1976) found in their study of heroin epidemics, during early phases of their addiction when getting high is still exciting, illicitly adventurous, and without the considerable burdens that it is capable of delivering over time. Based on his research on the spread of injection drug use among members of the working class in Madrid, Spain, for example, Juan Gamella notes that the transmission of knowledge about how to inject drugs tends to flow among "friends, neighbors, schoolmates, and even relatives" (1994:139).

In some cases, addiction is multigenerational, like a curious family heirloom or bad gene passed down through the generations, father to son, mother to daughter, or in some other pattern. This has been found occasionally to be the case with some multigenerational street gangs, where some of the children of the prior generation's members are "jumped into gang" (made members) when they come of age, including being introduced to the use of addictive drugs. In her sample of 80 Chicana heroin addicts, for example, Moore found that 11% first used heroin with a relative (1990:137). Usually in such instances, if somewhat strangely in light of just what it is that is being transmitted, a family member plays the role of teacher, helping neophyte drug users to overcome their fear while learning proper technique.

21

Research has shown that boys who identify with a drug-using father are more likely to use drugs themselves than are other boys (Brook et al. 1984; Milberger et al. 1999). In a study involving drug- and alcohol-involved fathers and their sons, we found that a father's abuse of alcohol with his son was highly predictive of adolescent drinking (Brook et al. 2003). This pattern may involve a number of factors, including the father role modeling problematic behaviors, communicating abusive drinking norms, as well as insuring the ready accessibility of alcohol in the home.

Other research has shown that a lack of closeness between a drug-abusing father and son predicts risky behavior in the son (Brook et al. 2002). This research has lead to the conclusion that an affectionate relationship between a father, even one who abuses drugs, and his son serves as a buffer against adolescent drug use. When such a bond does not exist, especially when the father–son relationship contains little in the way of affection and warmth and a lot in the way of control and punishment, the outlook for the son is not bright. Of course, some children seem to be innately resilient and can pass through bouts of parental physical and drug abuse as well as other misfortune without replicating similar negative patterns in their own lives. Tony was not one of those children, however.

EARLY YEARS: LIKE FATHER LIKE SON

In Tony's case, introduction to illicit drug injection came by way of his father, a morphine addict, who had also been introduced to drug injection by his own father many years earlier. According to Tony, like father like son:

> His father taught him the same thing. So, he was only teaching me what he knew best. He wanted me to be like him and I ended up being like him [an addict].

Precocious and independent, Tony had begun drug use the year before his life-long turn to drug injection was initiated, when, with groups of friends, he began drinking and using marijuana on an increasingly frequent basis. It was also at this time that he was first introduced to life in a street gang and to regular involvement in criminal acts, initially to have fun but eventually to pay for illicit drugs, a pattern that would define his life for many years thereafter. Participation in this netherworld on the edge of mainstream society began for Tony in the small, multi-ethnic, blue-collar city of Parkerton, Connecticut (pseudonym) (population approximately 70,000), where he was born. Like many of Connecticut's urban areas, poverty was common, unemployment high, and drugs were plentiful in Parkerton. And like the neighboring families in the housing project where he first lived, Tony's family—mother, father, son, and daughter—struggled to get by as best they could.

Not much really has changed in Tony's hometown since he was born there forty years ago. The 2000 census found that local per capita income was just over $18,000 a year and over 16% of the city's population lived below the federally established poverty line. Among children under 18 years of age who live there, about one-fourth live below the poverty line. One of the ironies of Connecticut is that its per capita income is the highest in the nation, but its cities, all of which are small in comparisons with the metropolises of New York, California, and elsewhere, are among the poorest in the country. Wealth in Connecticut, and an enormous amount of it, is largely concentrated along its aptly titled "Gold Coast" close to New York City—where homes commonly sell for $2 or $3 million, and $10-million homes can be easily found. Very little of that wealth, however, trickles down to the hinterland, to places like the projects of Parkerton. That is why, in Connecticut, it is always the best of times or the worst of times, depending on which side of the unlevel playing field you happen to be playing on as a result of who your parents happen to be.

In Tony's eyes, his mother was a saint, even though she ultimately rejected him because of his involvement with drugs, gangs, and delinquent ways. Like other men of his class background he could speak "in only the most deferential tones" about her (Gans 1962:63). Still, he is well aware that he never lived up to his mother's expectations. He notes:

> I have no religious beliefs. My mother is a Catholic, straight up religious fanatic. . . . I believe in God. I believe in Jesus. I believe if you don't believe in Jesus you ain't going to heaven. But, I haven't repented my sins. . . . I believe because . . . my mother taught me some, you know what I mean? She taught me every day about the bible stuff. But I don't believe in it like her. I don't wake up in the morning with a rosary in my hand. I haven't said some prayers in I don't know how long.

His feelings about his father, who he often described as a con man and a hustler, were more complex, if no less emotional, and filled as much with anger as with resignation, as much with acceptance as with disappointment.

These two poles in Tony's life came from two very different worlds, although both were from working-class families much closer to the bottom than the top of the American social hierarchy. They met when Tony's mother was only 16, a high school student volunteering in the local hospital as a "candy striper." She was from Connecticut, quite sheltered and innocent, a small attractive woman from a proud Italian family with old world traditions and tight social bonds. His father, by contrast, was 31, well over 6 feet tall, and a Korean War veteran of mixed Irish, French, and Native American ancestry, who had grown up on the mean streets of Philadelphia. He had been transferred from a veteran's hospital in Connecticut to the main hospital where Tony's mother was volunteering because of a war wound that became infected. Tony's father looked like a hero to the young hospital volunteer, and she could not hide her attraction. However, Tony recalls this is what his mother told him:

> My mother's father couldn't stand my father. He didn't like him 'cause he could see that he was a hood. He told my mother that he was a hood. But that made her want him more. . . . So they got married. He took her . . . now I know this part by heart. When they got married, this is what she told me, this is where the honeymoon [took place]. They went to Yankee Stadium and watched the Yankees play and bought a hot dog and some beer. . . . They [ate] at Jack Dempsey's restaurant 'cause my mother got [an] autograph. . . . She still had the autograph

from Jack Dempsey in Dempsey's restaurant. That was the honeymoon. That was the wedding 'cause they ran away. . . . They got married in Atlantic City. She was 16. Don't ask me how they got married but they did.

After the wedding in 1955, the couple settled in Connecticut near Tony's mother's family. Two years later, Tony's sister, Rachel was born. Tony came five years after that. When Tony was four, his family moved to Philadelphia, ostensibly to live closer to Tony's father's family. What Tony did not know at the time was that because of the pain of his war injury, Tony's father had developed a morphine habit (he also used heroin), mainlining the drug (i.e., injecting into a vein) daily to stay relatively pain-free and high. Moving to Philadelphia really was planned to improve Tony's father's access to drugs, for both personal use and for sale.

THE GOD OF DREAMS

Morphine is a derivative of opium (a substance long known to medicine), which is the milky sap secreted by the unripened seed-pod of the beautiful, flowering opium poppy plant (*Papaver somnifer*). The use of opium as a mood altering substance dates at least as far back as the ancient Middle Eastern Sumerian civilization, over 6,000 years ago.

The use of opium in the United States began during the colonial era. During the 18th and 19th centuries, it was sold legally over the counter in pharmacies and many other outlets as an ingredient in various tinctures, oils, and elixirs. By the end of the 18th century, a long list of patent medicines containing opium were readily available and widely used. While users became dependent on the drug, easy access limited the health and social consequences that we usually associate with drug addiction. Consequently, users, who came from many walks of life and included prominent people in society (but typically were White, middle class, and disproportionately women), were not condemned or penalized.

Morphine was discovered as a component of opium in 1803, during a series of experiments conducted by Frederick Wilhelm

Adam Serturner, in which he isolated the chief alkaloid in opium, a substance he named morphine, after Morpheus, the Greek god of sleep and dreams. Ten times more potent than raw opium, which Serturner knew directly because he used himself as a guinea pig, morphine was soon put to work as a painkiller by allopathic physicians; morphine, in fact, remains one of the strongest chemical pain relievers ever discovered. Even with the development of various synthetic painkillers, more than 200 tons of morphine are produced in the United States each year for relief among patients with acute or chronic pain and as a postoperative analgesic.

Morphine's painkilling capacity really gained attention during the Civil War, a conflict noted for producing enormous numbers of wounds that threatened to overwhelm the meager capacity of the mid-19th century allopathic medical system. In desperation, wartime physicians regularly used morphine to cope with war-inflicted wounds and limb amputations, gruesome products of the massive quantities of lead bullets and cannon balls fired by each side with deadly intentions in the direction of their adversaries. Battlefield use of morphine was aided by the timely invention of the hypodermic needle, which allowed the rapid movement of the potent drug through a vein and quickly to the brain, where it had its impact.

Of course, there was an important downside to morphine. It was highly addictive, and one product of its constant use during and after the war was the appearance of a brand new disease that, in fact, was soon named "soldier's disease"—it only developed among those who were wounded in the war and treated with morphine for pain, and who afterward had an intense craving for the drug as their primary symptom. By the end of the war, it is estimated that almost half a million people were suffering from this new iatrogenic disease. It has been estimated that during the war as many as 10 million opium pills were dispensed by doctors just to Union soldiers alone, along with almost 3 million ounces of other opium preparations that were also consumed medicinally. Indeed, the subsequent popularity of morphine created a non-medical market for syringes and related paraphernalia. Thus, the popular Sears Roebuck mail order catalogue at the end of the

19th century carried an advertisement for a hypodermic kit composed of a syringe, two detachable needles, two vials to hold morphine, and a carrying case, all for only $1.50. Like a cigarette lighter or beer mug, these were sold legally without reproach. Ultimately, nonmedical use of morphine was banned by the federal government. Medical use, however, which continues today, still produces a small number of patients with "soldier's disease," and Tony's father was one of them. His closest friends from his days in the military, people Tony's father would invite over for sit-down dinners, also were sufferers of this war disease, for which Tony's father offered the cure.

> Only dudes that would come over to the house . . . that would sit down, eat [dinner with the family], the morphine went with them. That was special. I don't know. It may have been people from the war or something but they were his buddies. It wasn't like they came in to cop [purchase drugs] and leave. They came in and stayed, drank, played cards. I used to see him shoot up.

DENIZENS OF HELL'S KITCHEN

In addition to his drug addiction, and intimately bound up with it, Tony's father was linked to a criminal gang called the Westies, one of last big-time Irish gangs that survived into the present era.

> He was 'um . . . not per se . . . a Westie but he used to hang with the Westies. With a couple of his friends from the service. . . . [He] knew a lot of guys in the service and when they got out, he started hanging with them in Philly and New York. He used to go to New York every weekend.

The Westies had emerged early in the 20th century on the Lower West Side of Manhattan in New York City, in the Hell's Kitchen area, and eventually spread to other locales sporting large Irish populations, including Philadelphia (English 1990, 2005). Legend has it that the area, featured in the graphically portrayed movie *Gangs of New York*, got its colorful nickname because of two police officers who were stationed there during the 19th century. Because of the intense poverty and resulting social tension and crime found there, one policeman referred to the area as Hell, to which the other allegedly responded, "This place is hotter then hell, its hell's kitchen."

While the term mob is often linked in popular imagination with the Italian Mafia or *La Cosa Nostra* (This Thing of Ours), Irish street gangs predate their more successful Italian counterparts—back to the massive migration of Irish to the United States during the years of British political and economic repression and the Irish potato famine. Upon their arrival in the New World, boatload after boatload of impoverished Irish refugees from the starving Irish countryside were cruelly preyed upon by first- and second-generation Americans, people who thought of themselves as "native" to what was, in fact, a land teeming with refugees. In response, the Irish formed their own street gangs to protect their neighborhoods; groups that once formed quickly turned to crime as a way to survive the grinding poverty of newcomer communities.

The Westies, in particular, developed a reputation for brutality and being trigger-happy, along with involvement in drug sales, robbery, loan sharking, and a long list of other crimes, both petty and profound. With the rise and ultimate domination of the U.S. criminal underworld by the Mafia, the Westies accepted their station in the netherworld and hired out as hit men to the stronger crime organization. Numerous members of the Westies were convicted of various crimes and incarcerated.

As best as Tony can recall, his father never had a "regular" job, a legitimate job, in his life. Rather he hustled and scammed. This included participation in robberies, break-ins, and related activities. As Tony put it, his father was involved in

> everything and anything. Gambling, some days was good and some days was bad. He never worked, never worked. And never had a regular job. He always used to come home . . . he wouldn't leave the house until five, six o'clock at night, come home at about four, five in the morning. He'd come home with 20 watches and money or he wouldn't come home with any-

thing. Most of the time he came home with money and other stuff . . . TVs, something. . . . [He did] everything from [running] numbers to scams. Anything that needed to be sold, because it was stolen, he knew where to do it.

Some of Tony's earliest memories were of his father socializing with Westie friends while drinking in bars for endless hours late into the night. The bar, in effect, was his father's home away from home and office, a place to enjoy friends and meet associates, a place to plan criminal activities and show respect to gang members of higher rank. At the same time, for Tony, it became a place of early socialization into the shadowy side of American life.

> From the time I was six or seven, he would take me with him to the bars where he would play pool and hang out and I would watch this man just come out playing pool like he was a shark, you know. And, my father, he used to say, "Watch me, you know, learn."

It appears likely that Tony's father suffered from a triple addiction: morphine, alcohol, and gambling. Multiple addictions of this sort are not uncommon. While tremendous concern has been expressed about illicit drug use and the dangers posed to society by street drug addicts, most studies of this population show that they also consume significant quantities of beer, wine, and hard liquor, and that many of their crimes occur while under the influence of alcohol. Research on addiction indicates that while addictive behavior patterns tend to coexist, and that all may involve self-medication for underlying emotional problems (Khantzian 1985, Khantzian, Mack, and Schatzberg 1974), different addictions may be addressing different "needs" in the sufferer.

For example, a recent Canadian study of pathological drinking and gambling, two behavioral patterns that commonly go hand-in-hand may be reactions to two quite different "needs" of sufferers (Tavares et al. 2005). While compulsive gamblers appear to be seeking stimulation to address feelings of depression, among alcoholics, strong anxiety was found to be the primary emotional need being addressed by pathological drinking. Research by Pearlin and Radabaugh on drinking, for example, indicates that anxiety is "especially likely to result in the use of alcohol as a tranquilizer if a sense of control is lacking and self-esteem is low" (1976:661). In that anxiety and depression also are commonly found together, it is not surprising that abusive drinking and gambling are as well.

Interestingly, research has begun to show that individuals who abuse drugs (especially the opiates) may be particularly intolerant of pain (although whether this is cause or consequence of drug abuse is not yet clear). What the research demonstrates is that the ratio of pain-sensitive to pain-tolerant individuals is considerably higher among drug abusers than other populations, when the same method of pain measurement is used (namely the cold pressor test, which involves the ability to withstand submerging your hand in ice water) (Compton 1994, Compton, Charuvastra, Kintaudi, and Ling, 2000). This research suggests that once exposed to pain-deadening drugs, individuals who are pain intolerant may be the most likely to develop an addiction. In other words, far from a moral shortcoming—of the sort that commonly elicits blame and social condemnation—drug addiction may be one expression of biological diversity in our species, much like having a high susceptibility to diabetes or other chronic diseases.

Although Tony never knew the precise source, his father had regular access to morphine; indeed, he recalled that his father could readily "score" (purchase) both hospital-grade morphine and heroin in bulk for resale to his friends and on the street:

> A lot of morphine, 'cause he was selling that to a lot of veterans. They were hooked on it. He told me that the heroin [then] really wasn't like it is now. You had to really know somebody for your dope. But when you did . . . that's why you went to New York and you got a connect [a drug source] out there. . . . It is easy to steal from a hospital. If you know somebody and you pay him the right amount of money, they'll do it with the keys. Even the doctors used [morphine] there. There's a lot of doctors down there [New York] that'll write you a scrip [prescription for morphine] for a hundred dollars. . . . He used to get it from a connection down there. He used to get morphine in a package, already in the vial.

BREAKING THE FAMILY CIRCLE

Tony recalled that as he was approaching his 10th birthday, tensions were building in his household. His parents began to argue, and the confrontations became more and more threatening. Even as a young boy, however, despite intensifying friction in his home, Tony took comfort in the fact that at least his father never hit his mother. Based on a study of families of different social classes, Lillian Rubin observes, "'He's a steady worker; he doesn't drink; he doesn't hit me'—these are the three attributes working-class women tick off most readily when asked what they value most in their husbands" (1976:93). It may be that Tony's mother did not believe that getting only one out of three of these desired traits was adequate. Perhaps this is why, when it came to striking her spouse, Tony's mother—who Tony once referred to as "a tough bird"—did not always show similar restraint in how she treated her husband, especially when it involved protecting Tony from his father's explosive temper, a mood that was exacerbated, in fact, by his father's abusive drinking and drug use.

> He never hit her, he never hit her. He used to swear at her but he never touched her or my sister. He treated my sister like a little princess. Like if she did something bad, she would blame me and automatically he would hit me without any questions. She didn't do no wrong [in their father's eyes], so he would hit me. But he would always have a shouting match with my mother. He would like . . . they call it now, verbally abuse her. I mean he would call her names and stuff. But he never touched her. I would just get the whippin'. . . . That was like on a daily basis. I mean he'll call her the B word. That is why I can't call a woman that 'cause I would hear that every day. . . . I mean say if the food was not ready or the ironing, you know, that's when he would get mad. If he got a phone call and he didn't like the way that it went, he would take it out on her. Or if he was mad at me, he'd whip me and yell at her 'cause I did something wrong. Stuff like that. I mean she didn't let that ride. There were times he would come in high and swear at her and there was one incident [in which] she threw a toaster at him. My

mother wasn't afraid of nothing. She threw a toaster at him and a couple of occasions she's the one that got physical with him, with knives. . . . She threw a couple of knives at him. There was this one incident at the [kitchen] table, he told her: "You bitch, this food sucks." She took a fork and he had a scar like this [motion with his hands]. Or if I did something wrong and he would hit me with a stick or a mop, you know my mother was tough. You know, she was a saint, a church lady, but when it came down to being tough, she was tough.

The constant bickering and increasingly more-intense fighting became routine for Tony. While it upset him, the mere certainty that it would happen became something, however ultimately painful it might have been, that he could depend on.

After a while, you get immune to it. It's like if it doesn't happen you wonder what's going on. Like on holidays, when the family came over, you know, uncles and cousins, they didn't start arguing until they left, you know, it wasn't in front of anybody. But like I said, even holidays wasn't immune to the arguing. But they loved each other. I know they did 'cause he would never touch her. But she would throw things at him, and I can understand. It hit him in the head and he wouldn't even touch her.

By contrast, Tony's father, a tall, muscular man who weighed over 300 pounds, did not hesitate to vent his anger on Tony.

My father wasn't much of a father to me. . . . He would hit me three or four times a day when I was younger for teasing my sister or slapping her or if my mother said I was bad. . . . Some days when I was younger, it would be spanking . . . or use a belt or go get a switch. Sometimes he would tell me to go get one and I would try to get the driest one and whenever I did that it would be worse and [he'd use] a belt. Then after, as I got older, I'd be fighting him [back], you know, after he tried to hit me. I would hit him back toward the end. [He'd] chase after me. After awhile, I couldn't take it, I would run out of the house. I mean like twice a week for real bad ones, [he's] chasing me. Half the time, I didn't know what I did. But other times it would be light, you know, a little spanking, "why did you hit your sister?"

Whether it was the constant fighting and verbal abuse, or his father's growing involvement in drugs or perhaps his dismal track record as a family provider or even his hanging out, constantly gambling and drinking in bars with friends and fellow hustlers, or all of these combined, when Tony was 10 years old his parents divorced. His mother, with Tony and his sister in tow, returned to Connecticut to be close to her family, the only support she had left in the world. Financially, however, she was on her own and without job skills or a work history. Still, she managed as best she could by working two low-paying jobs and by depending on Tony's sister to provide supervision for her younger brother.

> My mother came back to [Connecticut] and lived in the [housing] projects, so I came with her. But, as I was growing up . . . I was startin' to hang around with the kids over there [in the projects] and we were tearing up. I was hanging around with the older kids so my mother sent me back to my father to straighten me out. That's when he started involving me with his hustling and all that.

OMENS OF THINGS TO COME

It was during the time he was living in the housing projects of Parkerton that Tony joined his first street gang, a group inauspiciously called the Omens, and it was through his involvement with fellow gang members that he began drinking and experimenting with psychotropic drugs, including, as he put it: "nothing hard. I mean, a little cocaine we snorted, but that was about it." Like many kids his age living in impoverished inner-city neighborhoods across the United States, street gangs are a fact of life, as common and expectable as soccer teams and ballet lessons among suburban youth. Tony recalls:

> I was starting drinking, gettin' high with weed, and 'um, we had that little gang, Omens. . . . We called it Omens. But we'd go around, breakin' in cars, go into school, fightin' with the other kids. . . . My mother couldn't handle it and my sister, she was like a baby . . . 'cause my mother, she was workin' two jobs. So

she was hardly there so, she left my sister there to watch me. And my sister was doin' her thing. She was gettin' high on weed and havin' her friends over. So I would be out all night, 10, 12 years old. Goin' around the projects, knockin' on doors, spray-painting doors, you know, little kid stuff. And then fightin', breakin' windows in cars, stealin' radios. . . . That's how we started. And my mother just couldn't handle it anymore. I would come home drunk, high, act foolish.

In response to the growing number of American youth who become involved in street gangs—estimates are that there are over 800,000 youth in street gangs in the United States—social science researchers have examined the individual and social characteristics of youth who join gangs (compared with those of similar age from the same general area who do not join). In a Seattle study, for example, Karl Hill (1999) and his colleagues tracked 808 fifth-grade students (approximately 10 or 11 years of age) attending 18 elementary schools located in higher-crime neighborhoods beginning in the fall of 1985. These youth were followed prospectively until 1993, when they were all 18 or so years of age.

The participants in the study were interviewed annually about their life situation, conditions in their home and neighborhoods, their attitudes, involvement with alcohol and drugs, and participation in street gangs. These researchers found that a range of factors from every domain of the youths' experience, including neighborhood characteristics, family attributes and behavior, school factors, peer relations, and individual personality factors all predicted gang affiliation. They found that:

> The strongest predictors at ages 10 to 12 were the availability of marijuana in the neighborhood, [living in] neighborhoods [where many] youth [were] in trouble, living with one parent . . . having initiated marijuana use [at a young age], having engaged in violence, low academic achievement, and being identified as learning disabled in school. (Hill et al. 1999:305)

These finding replicate those of other studies that also note the importance of residence, family structure, poverty, low academic aspirations, having delinquent peers, early participation in delinquent behaviors, and early use of alcohol and other drugs (Decker and Van-Winkle 1996, Hagedorn 1994a, 1994b, Spergel and Curry 1993).

In addition, the findings of Hill and his coworkers especially emphasize the importance of neighborhood factors, like living in an area where many youth are engaged in behaviors that get them trouble with the police or at school, where it is relatively easy for youth to acquire drugs and alcohol, and where pre-adolescent and adolescent antisocial behavior is common. Simply put, place matters. Moreover, they found that exposure to a greater number of these kinds of risk factors in childhood greatly increased the likelihood of joining a youth gang.

Certainly this configuration of factors fairly well describes Tony's situation at age 10. He was living with only one of his parents in a low-income, high-crime neighborhood in which delinquent behavior was all but normative among youth, drugs and alcohol could be had easily, and school was seen among peers more as punishment than as a place of learning and personal development. Rather than a school- or family-orientation, Tony developed a strong street- and peer-orientation that contributed to the appeal of gangs as well as delinquent activities that on some level expressed rejection of conventional society, adult authority, and mainstream values.

Ultimately, Tony's ever more unruly behavior—which no doubt reminded Tony's mother of her ex-husband—led to her difficult decision to send Tony back to Philadelphia to live with his father and his father's relatives. Even now, Tony notes:

> I don't have a relationship with my mother. . . . I see her sometimes but it seems like when she looks at me, she looks at my father, or sometimes the way I act [reminds her] and she can't stand that. . . . There is no love there. . . . You know, she lets me know about it. So I just don't go there any more.

The rationale for sending Tony to Philadelphia, ironically, was that his mother felt that he needed a firmer hand, an adult who could control him and curb his delinquent ways. Thus at age 10 Tony returned to the City of Brotherly Love, although he found very little of that emotion as he resumed his life in his former hometown.

Once back in Philadelphia, with one foot already over the line of conventionality, Tony quickly moved into the underground world of illicit behavior, criminal involvement, and drug addiction, all before becoming a teenager, with limited experience of alternative ways of behaving, little exposure to the social world beyond two working-class neighborhoods, and hardly any direct awareness of mainstream values concerning education, careers, and stable family life. In short, Tony's slide into a lifetime of drug dependency, "gangbangin,'" hustling, and criminality was not a failure on his part, as he had little sense of what the wider society considered success or appropriate social behavior.

Moreover, even if he never dreamed the dreams of middle-class accomplishment while young—later, when the rigors of street life, a growing awareness of his own mortality, and an endless stream of social suffering began to wear him down and sap his confidence, he would come to dream such dreams often, even though conventional routes of social achievement were not readily available to him nor was he much aware of them. The people he knew and saw around him every day, in the projects and on inner-city urban street corners did not go to college, did not become doctors or engineers, did not buy homes in the suburbs and go on family vacations to Disney World, did not drive their grown children from city to city or even state to state in search of the perfect setting for the higher education of another generation, did not even feel valued or respected in society. Rather, they struggled and coped, and got by as best they could, even though some of what they did was condemned by those who led different lives in nicer homes in wealthier neighborhoods.

The understanding that life in those other, higher-status places among people with far greater social standing was made possible by the labor of the working class was deeply felt, if rarely articulated, by those at the bottom and certainly never acknowledged by those at the top of our class structured but class-denying society. Certainly, such ideas were not on Tony's mind. Rather, he learned to live day-by-day, grabbing what pleasure he could out of life, and illicit drugs, with their significant mood-altering capacity, were a readily available means of achieving this goal.

• Chapter 3 •

On the Prowl
Preteen Years

Youth mural

*[T]oday we live in a climate of heightened
risk awareness coupled with a nostalgia for
an imagined past in which children played safely
throughout a carefree innocent childhood.*

—Stevi Jackson and Sue Scott,
"Risk Anxiety and the Social Construction of Childhood"

*They're closing down the textile mill
across the railroad tracks,
Foreman says these jobs are going boys
and they ain't coming back,
to your hometown*

—Bruce Springsteen, "My Hometown"

THE POLITICAL ECONOMY OF LIFE

Tony never knew a carefree innocent childhood. Once his parents were divorced, he was much more at home on the street than in the home of either his mother in Connecticut or his father in Pennsylvania. Unable to reign in her son's increasingly wild and bellicose behavior, Tony's mother sent him off to live with his father, even though she was painfully aware of the latter's entwinement in a tumultuous world of illicit drugs, dishonest scams, and fast hustles. Still, whatever his shortcomings, Tony's mother knew that her ex-husband did not spare the rod or spoil the child. It was firm discipline, she convinced herself, that Tony most needed, and she sent him back to his father to get it. Helplessness, no doubt, often serves as the progenitor of desperate acts.

By the time Tony returned to Philadelphia, his father had remarried. His step-mother, who was Puerto Rican, had several brothers and nephews—individuals who would soon play an important role in Tony's life—who were heavily involved in drug use and related criminal activities. Tony's sister, by contrast, stayed with their mother in Connecticut, completed high school and went on to finish college, living a life quite different from her brother. After college, she took a position with an insurance company. Like her mother, however, she came to see Tony as more burden than brother, more disappointment than dependable sibling. She led her life, he led his.

It is not a coincidence that Tony's sister would develop a career in the insurance industry. Connecticut, in fact, is home to over 100 insurance companies—marine insurance, the grandfather of all modern brands of insurance was first developed in the state to cover the many ships and cargoes that set sail from the state's ocean and river ports. Connecticut was also the birthplace of other forms of insurance, products of industrial accidents and fires that plagued the rapidly industrialized state over 100 years ago. Indeed, it was Connecticut's prowess in industry that provided jobs to the thousands of dislocated *contandini* from southern Italy—peasants who flocked from places like Calabria, Salerno, Abruzzi, and Potenza to Connecticut at the end of the 19th and early 20th centuries, including, very likely, Tony's maternal grandparents.

In his book *Urban Change in Central Connecticut: From Farm to Factory to Urban Pastoralism* geographer David Meyer (1976) identified four factors that favorably disposed Connecticut to leap ahead in industrialization: (1) a tradition of technological innovativeness among its craftsmen; (2) a literate population; (3) a social and political climate that favored shrewdness and acquisitiveness; and (4) the availability of merchant capital that could be funneled into new industrial ventures. By the mid-19th century, tiny Connecticut ranked fourth among the nation's industrialized states.

By the time Tony was born, however, the industrial base of Connecticut, the foundation upon which several generations of working-class people, migrants from Ireland, Germany, Poland, Italy, and elsewhere in Europe, made their living, raised their families, and made themselves eventually into middle-class Americans, was rusting away. The deindustrialization of Connecticut began in the 1950s as factories that had boomed during the Second World War began to close down. Much of this production shifted to the South or overseas, and with it went the decent-paying, unionized manufacturing jobs of many of Connecticut's blue-collar workers, the descendents of past migrations. As a result, not only did Tony not have a carefree childhood, he had little prospect of acquiring the type of job that previously had provided stable employment and a foothold in the mainstream American lifestyle for boys like him. Instead, like many of his peers and other youth to follow after him on Connecticut's inner-city streets, he wandered aimlessly along another path, one that ultimately spiraled downward into addiction, imprisonment, and disease.

STREET YOUTH

Once back in Philadelphia, and under the supervision of a father who spent his days drinking, playing pool, and engaging in scams and hustles of various sorts, Tony quickly replicated his prior pattern with the Omens and fell in with a rough group of neighborhood friends. As for school, he reported:

> School didn't interest me because there was no money there at that time. I made more money on the street . . . I was in and out [of school]. I was attempting to go. I stayed [in school] . . . I think it was the ninth grade. Even then, I would only go to hang out in the halls.

Out of school, Tony spent his days hanging out with friends.

> I was big and I used to hang with older kids. I used to handle myself with them. I used to fight them too sometimes. . . . Where I lived down there, it's a mixed neighborhood. . . . Nobody cared about colors down there. . . . Grow up with everybody down there—it's no big deal the color you were. If you were Black, White, Puerto Rican or even Vietnamese. Nobody there cares as long as you hang out together in the street and you watched each other's back, no problem.

Tony's circle of local friends was regularly engaged in adolescent turf wars with the kids who lived on nearby streets. To make money in Philadelphia, they specialized in beating up and robbing students from the local university.

> All my friends from our street, we used to go to the next street and fight with them [the neighboring boys] or go down to Temple University and throw rocks at [the students] to try to get them to chase us. When they chased us, we'd beat them up and rob them. . . . That's how we used to hang out down there. We had knives; nobody had guns.

In addition, they would shoplift from local stores, rob money from hot dog vendors on the street, and, when the opportunity arose, break into homes to steal what they could. One day, Tony recalled, they developed a plan to shoplift from a store.

We went into the store one day. It was old, a mom and pop store, you know. Freddy and I went in to shoplift. All of a sudden, Freddy decides to pull out a gun and tell the old woman to give me the money. We're looking at Freddy like: "Yo, you crazy man?" So we ran out of the store and I don't know exactly what happened, where this person came from, but all of a sudden we heard a shot and . . . Freddy was shot in the shoulder. Freddy didn't have no bullets in his gun. He had a gun but no bullets. It was rusted out. He just wanted to get the lady . . . to give him the money, but she's not the one that shot him, it was her nephew. . . . We didn't even know he was there. . . . We ran after we seen Freddy on the ground because we went there to shoplift and Freddy pulled a gun. We ain't want no part of that. . . . Freddy went to juvi [juvenile detention center] and I never seen him since.

A few years later, Tony was involved in another shooting, this one with tragic results. The incident began when he was walking down the street with his friend Carlito, when they encountered a group of youth from a rival neighborhood.

Some words were passed and all of a sudden this guy pulls out a gun and shoots Carlito right here [points to heart]. Carlito dropped to the ground. Everybody ran, but I stayed with him. Someone called the ambulance. Two of the ambulances came and I stayed with him. I tried to keep him breathing 'cause he would stop, he would like start breathing hard. And this was the first time I had to experience that, somebody dying on you, right in your hands. I mean, he died holding my hand. . . . During the time he was breathing heavy, he had like a sad look on his face but when he held my hand tightly he stopped breathing. Like he smiled for a minute. That scared the hell out of me . . .

As a result of this experience, Tony began to worry about dying.

When I was younger, I used to be scared to die. I used to go to sleep scared that I was gonna die. I would sit there with my eyes open [thinking] "please, I don't want to die God."

After Carlito died, Tony's cousin Alex was shot in a drive-by shooting. Another cousin ran to find Tony and tell him what had happened to Alex.

I had just come around the corner after everything happened. Somebody was laying on the ground. . . . That's when he died. He told me he loved me. I tried, you know, I tried to ask him who did it and he didn't have enough time to tell me who did it. But we found out who did it. Everything was straight on that. . . . A month later they found that individual that shot Alex, they found him dead in the neighborhood. So everything was straight.

Tony never told me who killed Alex's murderer. He certainly didn't admit to being involved but remained ambiguous about what happened and who was involved. Very likely, since he would later admit to participation in similar acts, he did not commit the murder but knew who did. And very likely, it was someone in his father's circle of friends and relatives, a crew that was not likely to take the murder of a kinsman lightly.

Then, another friend got shot when he tried to rob a man in a bar.

He got shot in the side. He was running from this guy 'cause he ripped him off in a bar. He was running down the street and he got shot right here [pointing to his left side under his armpit]. The bullet was like a tumbler. It came through here and just tumbled down and nicked the heart bad enough he could have died from that. I wasn't right there. I wasn't holding him. Because when that happened, we all scattered. When the bullets started flying, I had my girlfriend with me and I was on top of her on the ground making sure a stray bullet if it comes its gonna hit me before it hits her.

In yet another incident:

My friend was in a bar, drunk and he walked out and this other individual walked out of the bar drunk too and they had words. When I had came out of the bar, all of a sudden I seen this guy is standing over my friend taking a knife out of him. I don't know if it hit his heart, but he died instantly. I chased the man but he got in a car and left. I called the police. My first reaction should have been to call the police, but I chased him. I was gonna kill this individual.

In short, starting in his preteen years, Tony was no stranger to violence, brutal street violence that took a painful toll on those who were close to him and, ultimately, on his psyche as well.

ENTER DOPE

The sudden tragic death of friends and relatives was not all of the woe that befell Tony during this period. Within a few years of returning to Philadelphia, he began his enduring involvement with heroin. Drugs, of course, were not new to Tony; introduction to them had come so early in his life he was hardly able to exercise good judgment in deciding whether or not to use them. He did what his friends did and believed like them that drugs were fun, adventurous, indeed, a carefree escape from life in the projects. Tony's uncle, his father's brother and a member of his father's crew of hustlers and drug dealers, played a significant role in his "graduation" from alcohol and marijuana to regular use of harder drugs and before long to addiction. Tony's consequential journey into this world began when his father told him that to earn his keep he had to help his uncle on the street selling dope.

Tony's first job in the dope trade, at age 13 and not long after he dropped out of school, was as a "runner," ferreting bags of heroin as needed from the place where they were hidden to his uncle's selling spot on the street corner. Then he would run the profits over to his father in the bar.

> When my mother sent me back to my father, that's when the dope [heroin] started . . . 'cause I started gettin' high with my uncle. When we were out on the corner [selling], I seen him crack a bag, you know . . . 'cause I was just helpin' him, you know. When he would run out, I would go get him some more. But I seen him crack open somethin' and sniff it.

To show Tony what was in the little plastic bags he was helping his uncle to sell on the street, he was given "a taste." This he snorted up his nose, as he had seen his uncle do, a common "starter" method in the consumption of heroin. Many people who begin snorting the drug or perhaps skin-popping it (injecting under the skin or into a muscle), later go on to mainlining it to rapidly experience the full drug effects (as the blood system swiftly moves it through the body, it passes the blood/brain barrier and reaches the brain within about 10 seconds after injecting, producing a profound impact on the user's experience).

Tony quickly came to enjoy snorting heroin. As he recalled, "I was gettin' high, that's all I knew. It made me feel good." After Tony had been snorting heroin for several weeks, he woke up one morning feeling quite ill.

> I was throwin' up. I had, you know, diarrhea at that time. My father wanted to know what was going on. And then I told him I used to watch [uncle] Buster crack open and sniff, and I sniffed too; that's when my dad got mad. . . . That's when he shot me up. He thought it was gonna scare me away from gettin' high. Well, I guess psychologically it was supposed to turn me off. But it did not work that way. . . . Then he said, "Well, you gonna be a junkie, you might as well be a good one." He shot me up at 13 and I have been flying ever since.

"Flying" as Tony called it, or being high as it is generally known on the street, is caused by the way heroin interacts with brain cells and brain chemistry. In the brain, heroin is converted into morphine and binds with natural opiate receptors. These are locations in the brain that chemically recognize drugs of the opiate family, including the endorphins, which are opiate chemicals that are found naturally in the brain and are released in response to pain and stress. Running is probably enjoyable to joggers, in part, because it also releases such drugs in the brain. At opiate receptor sites, which are located in areas of the brain that function primarily to regulate pain, breathing, and the emotions, as well as in the central nervous system, heroin depresses the transmission of nerve impulses that signal pain. Having the ability to eliminate pain, and the emotions attached to it, makes heroin a powerful substance. Moreover, the drug relieves anxiety, calms muscles, causes drowsiness, and produces a sense of well-being and contentment.

Heroin is so addictive because the brain quickly builds up a tolerance to its presence and ever-larger doses must be used to produce the same pain-deadening and euphoric effects. The body literally comes to crave the drug and failure to meet this demand sets off a painful process of withdrawal including chills, cramps, sweats, and a general sense of misery, avoidance of which is compelling for most users. At this point, the user is addicted, which is often a turning pointing, influencing many subsequent events in his/her life.

Individual reaction to one's first exposure to heroin varies greatly. For some, it is like falling in love; it's an experience that users describe in quite romantic terms, leading to a long-term quest to relive the initial euphoric experience. For example, for poet Piri Thomas, the power of heroin to wash away all of the pain and rejection he had known prior to his first encounter with the drug made it instantly appealing: "All your troubles become a bunch of bleary blurred memories . . ." (Thomas 1967:200). Early in his use of the drug, this was Tony's experience as well:

> Heroin. Straight heroin. It's like it runs through my veins. You know, you can have a girlfriend with dope, it's like your wife. . . . It's like it calls to me. . . . It's like I am in love with it. I'm in love with heroin more than I am with a woman. I give everything to heroin. It's crazy but it's true. I use heroin first not to be sick [from withdrawal] and the rest of the day trying to chase that high to feel no pain in my body.

Others have rather different first experiences. Writer Claude Brown, who like Tony first snorted heroin at age 13, has written that his first heroin high started off gloriously.

> I couldn't believe it was really happening. I almost wanted to break out and laugh for joy, but I held back, and I snorted. . . . Something hit me right in the top of the head. It felt like a little spray of pepper on my brain. . . . Everything was getting rosy, beautiful. The sun got brighter in the sky and the whole day lit up and was twice as bright as it was before. . . . Everything was so slo-o-ow. (Brown 1965:110–111)

The pleasant part of the experience faded quickly, however, and things grew dark and threatening as more heroin reached the synapses in Brown's brain.

> My head seemed to stretch, and I thought my brain was going to burst. It was like a headache taking place all over the head at once and trying to break its way out. And then it seemed to get hot and hot and hot. And I was so slow... I got scared. I'd never felt this way before in my life. . . . My guts felt like they were going to come out. Everything was bursting out all at once, and there was nothing I could do. . . . And I said, "O Lawd, if you'll just give me one more chance, one more chance, I'll never get high again." (Brown 1965:111)

In Brown's case, while he did use other drugs for a time, his first encounter with heroin was his last. That was not the case with Tony; rather, like for Piri Thomas and many other first-time users, it was the beginning of a dream that started off warm and sweet but over time became a seemingly endless and punishing nightmare that proved impossible to escape for long.

THE HISTORY OF H

Heroin like morphine, and like a growing number of now illicitly used substances, came into the world in a laboratory. A British chemist named C. R. A. Wright began carrying out a series of exploratory experiments during the 1870s that involved combining morphine with various acids. One of the chemicals Wright discovered thereby was a compound he christened diacetylmorphine. Twenty-four years later, a German pharmacologist named Heinrich Dreser, who headed the pharmaceutical lab of the Bayer Company—a former dye manufacturer that grew into the first of the "Big Pharm" drug corporations—used Wright's chemical in a series of his own experiments.

Dreser, who had a hand in the development of aspirin (a drug that now has a sales volume of 40 billion tablets a year), was responsible for testing the safety and effectiveness of new Bayer drugs. He was one of the first pharmacologists, in fact, to test drugs on animals on a large scale before human testing began.

Thus in 1898 he started testing diacetylmorphine on stickleback fish, frogs, and rabbits. He then tested the drug on some of his fellow Bayer workers as well as on himself. The reaction among his laboratory staff was most positive, and they reported that it made them feel heroic, thus giving the drug its popular name.

Dreser next administered diacetylmorphine to a sample of human subjects who were suffering from a range of maladies. He reported that diacetylmorphine proved to be very effective in the treatment of coughs, chest pains, and other discomforts associated with various respiratory diseases. Antibiotics were unknown at the time, and respiratory diseases like tuberculosis and pneumonia were the leading causes of death in the Western world. To his joy, Dreser discovered that diacetylmorphine was even more effective than morphine or codeine for treating respiratory problems, and he drew the erroneous conclusion that a fatal overdose of diacetylmorphine was not possible.

The Bayer laboratory was soon marketing its new wonder drug under the upbeat trade name of Heroin, which was derived from the German word for heroic (heroisch). Before long, Heroin was being widely promoted as a nonaddictive cure for morphine addiction. As a Bayer advertisement from this era stated: Heroin is "free from unpleasant after effect," a polite euphemism for drug addiction (in Inciardi 1986:10). This grievous error occurred because morphine addicts who were going through painful withdrawal stopped experiencing all of their symptoms when they were given Heroin. At the time, people did not understand the phenomenon we now call "cross-addiction" (i.e., addiction to one opiate produces addiction to all opiates).

To launch the new wonder drug, thousands advertisements and free samples of the drug were mailed by Bayer to physicians across Europe and the United States. Within a few years, Bayer was selling a ton of Heroin a year, with exports to over 20 countries. It became especially popular in the United States, where patent medicines were widely sold and drug laws were all but nonexistent. Given its seemingly lofty attributes and the extensive advertisement boost it received, Heroin was soon a very accepted and increasingly commonly used legal drug.

Bayer continued to manufacture and sell Heroin until 1913, by which time its addictive properties had become well known. The following year purchase of the drug without a prescription was banned in the U.S., and within another five years doctors were barred from prescribing it to their patients. The banning of Heroin was part and parcel of a wider effort to restrict psychotropic drug use in the United States. While the users of these substances had once been neighbors, friends, business associates, and kinsmen, they came to be socially redefined "as a kind of threatening 'other' whose actions and lifestyles undermined the structure of mainstream society" (Page 2004:377). Ironically, "tobacco, by far the most important killer among all drugs, slipped under the scrutiny of those who would police drug use in the world" (Page 2004:377).

Heroin, of course, did not disappear once its use was outlawed, rather it went underground becoming an illicit street drug imported and sold by various criminal groups under an array of colorful street names including smack, dope, horse, jive and H. Supplies tended to come from two sources: countries in which poppy cultivation was legal and traffickers were able to siphon off a percentage of the crop for illicit processing, and countries where poppy growing officially was illegal but the government was not strong enough to control cultivation, even, as has happened in recent years, with massive inputs of fiscal, technological, and military aid through the U.S. War on Drugs (Booth 1996).

The initial users of illicit heroin were individuals who had become addicted while it was still legal, but in time new users flocked to the drug and soon outnumbered those who had once used it legally. By the 1930s, an underground subculture of heroin users had emerged, and it has flourished ever since, despite ups and downs in the availability, cost, and quality of the product being sold. Currently it is estimated that there are a million heroin addicts in the U.S. alone, and the drug continues to spread worldwide, even in the midst of the AIDS epidemic, to which—both because of the sharing of injection drug equipment among users and having unprotected sex under the disinhibiting effects of heroin—it has contributed greatly with tragic results. In northeastern cities like Hartford, many heroin injectors were infected early in the epidemic, leading to rates of infection in this population that approached 50% prior to the implementation of prevention efforts that have since contributed significantly to a decline in the levels of HIV infection among contemporary heroin addicts. Tony, however, as has been his life pattern, was not among the lucky ones who somehow dodged the bullet of HIV infection or other blood-borne diseases associated with illicit injection.

HARSH LESSONS

Within two years of going to live with his father, an incident happened that marked that beginning of Tony's numerous brushes with the law.

> My cousin took my father's gun out of the house and I caught him. We were wrestling over it outside and the gun went off. Nobody got hurt or anything. But the police came. Even though it was my father's gun, I said we stole the gun out of a car. I went to juvi [juvenile detention] for two years I think for that. I could have said it was his, but he had no permit. So I went to jail for him. But it wasn't so bad in juvi. They made you go to school all day. Weekends you could play outside. The older kids were trying to be like mobsters, but I didn't pay them no mind.

When he was released Tony visited his mother, visited old friends from the Omens, but soon returned to Philadelphia to live with his father. Seeing that his son was now more experienced, Tony's father assigned him a street corner of his own from which to peddle the heroin. Tony would spend his day dispensing the little plastic bags to a steady stream of needy customers, and return home at the end of shift to give the proceeds to his father. Notes Tony:

> He had me. I was out there [on the street]. I used to sell bundles for him. Back then, it was like thirty dollars a bag. . . . See, I was scared of my father at that time. . . . If I were to come back short [with less money than he was suppose to have made

given the number of bags of heroin he had been given to sell], I
would get a whippin'. He would beat my ass. . . . He broke my
nose a couple times with punches. . . . You know what I mean?
You can't come back short. . . . He used to beat me if I would
come back short of if I didn't do things the way he wanted it
done. . . . He kept saying this was gonna toughen me up.

Then one day, when Tony was 15, an addict tried to rob him
of his dope profits, a common risk faced by those who peddle
drugs on the streets. Tony's father was outraged that someone
would try to steal his money or drugs. To protect his operation
from theft, he gave Tony a gun.

This guy tried to rip me off, and my father, at that time, he gave
me his gun. He said, "if you need to use it, use it." Then
[another] man tried to rip me off and that's when I shot him. I
shot a man over. . . fifty dollars. I was 15. He died. . . . I was
more afraid of being robbed and coming home short that I
killed this individual. I was that scared of my father. . . . I mean,
I still get flash backs til this day about that. I mean, I took a
man's life for fifty dollars. But back then it was like if I didn't do
that and he would have took my money, I was more scared of
my father. This individual, he came up and said he wanted 10
bags of dope, I gave it to him and he said, "I'm not going to pay
you." The man had a gun and he pulled the gun out. He shot
and I shot. Luckily I only got a flesh wound in my leg. But I
killed him. I shot him in the head. . . . He died at the
hospital. . . . I knew him. He was a rip-off artist.

Tony was struck by his father's reaction when he heard that
his son had shot and killed another man.

To be honest with you, he was proud of me. . . . He smiled and
said, "Now you are a man" 'cause I took another man's life. I
mean, if I did anything like he would do, he would be proud.
But if I did anything that wasn't like him, he was . . . kind of
dissatisfied, even if it turned out to be good for me. If he
wouldn't do it, he was more dissatisfied at that. [With the kill-
ing] somehow I gained more respect with him.

GUILTY

Although only 15, Tony was tried as an adult for the shooting. Found guilty, he was imprisoned in the state penitentiary and served seven years behind bars. During the time Tony went to prison, the number of people incarcerated in the U.S. had begun to soar. The War on Drugs was primarily responsible for this sudden and massive increase in the number of people serving prison sentences. Central to the legislative agenda in the War on Drugs has been an effort to significantly increase penalties for drug-related offenses, coupled with funding for local police departments and federal forces to arrest continually more people on drug charges. From 1980 until 2003, the number of state and local drug-related arrests almost tripled to a high of 1,678,000 (Bureau of Justice Statistics, 2005), while the rate of drug arrests per 100,000 population jumped from 288 to 726 (The Sentencing Project 2005). Due to the War on Drugs there has been a rapid growth in the number of female inmates, which is currently 103,310. Despite the fall in the crime rate in the United States, the continuous rise in the number of inmates—currently approximately one out of every 138 Americans—places the United States first, compared to other countries. Even rural jails have filled up with individuals charged with drug offenses (Kane and Dotson 1997).

As a result of these dramatic developments, even the former "drug czar" of the U.S., General Barry McCaffrey, during an interview on the TV program *CBS This Morning,* which aired on September 13, 1999, criticized the extraordinary number of drug offenders in the criminal justice system saying that we have erected a "drug gulag." While Tony was not charged with a drug offense, the fact that he was selling drugs when he committed murder contributed significantly to his handling in the criminal justice system. He was armed, violent, and a drug peddler, a toxic combination that overwhelmed any sympathy or understanding that might have been evoked by his young age or how it was that he came to be selling drugs in the first place. Tony had become the bogeyman of modern America, the monster that hides beneath the bed of our cultural ideology of good and bad, right and wrong, honor and evil. We have invested billions of dollars constructing places for "people like Tony" where they can languish in misery behind cold steel bars contemplating their crimes against society.

Beyond the War on Drugs, another force pushing for prison expansion is the increasingly well-heeled prison lobby. In his last presidential speech to the nation before leaving office, President Dwight D. Eisenhower, a man generally seen as a social conservative, and certainly one with considerable experience with the military, having served as the head of Allied forces during World War II, warned of the rise of a military-industrial complex in the United States. By this term, Eisenhower referred to a cozy alignment that had formed between branches of the U.S. government, especially the Pentagon, and several corporations involved in the weapons-production industry and the related supplying of military needs. Pointing to the "potential for the disastrous rise of misplaced power," Eisenhower feared that these two dominant sectors of our society, if united, would be so overwhelming that the interests of the military-industrial complex—such as always constantly pushing for military buildup and even war—would be put above the needs of the country and the will of the people and their elected officials. Some have argued that the constant involvement of the U.S. in wars across the face of the globe since Eisenhower's presidency is confirmation of his vision.

With something of the same notion in mind, some people have begun to warn about the rise of a prison-industrial complex involving an alliance between existing prisons around the country, private prison operators anxious to open a new "franchise," and corporations that supply the prison system with needed commodities and products or profit from products produced at sub-minimum wages in prison-based factories. In the eyes of a growing number of critics, the prison-industrial complex has evolved a powerful lobby that is committed to pressing for the construction of new prisons, renovation of old prisons, and the expansion of existing prisons so as to keep profits up. To fill these prisons, so that the public does not think of them as wasted expenditures, the prison-industrial complex must push for more stringent laws and greater punishment. As Arnold Chien, Margaret Connors, and Kenneth Fox observe, "There is good reason to believe that the burgeoning prison industry, like any other big industry will emerge as an obstacle to any policy initiatives which interfere with its prerogatives" (2000:318). This is relatively easy to do because it is always possible to play on an existing cultural theme and accuse reformers of being "soft on crime," a dangerous label for any politician who wants to be re-elected in a society that feels ever-vulnerable and at the mercy of wanton street criminals.

Under such circumstances, it is the needs of the prison-industrial complex and not those of society—which understandably wants less crime but not necessarily more prisoners—that come to drive the country's penal agenda. In the view of a former warden at the Oklahoma State Reformatory, for example, "The War on Drugs is a failure and a success. It's a failure because it has not stopped drug use in this country. It's a success because it's the best economic boom we've ever seen. Prisoners are big business. It's [a] . . . growth industry . . . and the profits are overriding expenses" (quoted in Chien et al. 2000:319).

The problem, of course, is that although incarceration gets criminals off of the streets for a time—at steep cost to taxpayers—almost all prisoners eventually serve their time and, like Tony, go back to doing what they were doing before they were arrested, but with new ideas for how to succeed, new partnerships with other criminals, and new skills in illicit behaviors. Additionally, many also return to the streets with new infections—like HIV and hepatitis—all of which have consequences for the communities that receive them.

As a teenage "fish" (a new prisoner) in an adult prison, Tony, like other younger prisoners, quickly attracted the lascivious attention of older inmates who saw an opportunity to take sexual advantage of the new inmate. He was, like author Piri Thomas' friend Ricardo, who entered prison at age 14, "perfect prey for the jailhouse wolves" (1991:264). Recalls Tony:

> I was a target every day until I proved myself. I had to prove myself every day. . . . There were these Black guys and they

tried to rape me. I had an uncle and several cousins [through his step-mother] there for drugs, and when one of the guys who tried to rape me came around the corner, he was killed. I did it. They held him down on the ground and my uncle said, "Kill the Nigger," and I did. My uncle Tomás was going to do it but he asked me if I wanted to do it because he seen the rage in my eyes. My uncle was carrying a shank [homemade knife] made of a piece of wood and a nail. I stabbed him with it. My uncle took the rap for that because he was in for life, but people [other inmates] knew who did it. After awhile the attempted rapes stopped. People started giving me respect.

For once, fortune smiled upon Tony and he was never charged for the second murder. Had he been convicted, he would not have gotten out of prison for decades. As it was, he served seven years for the first murder, a period during which he adapted to prison life so completely that he would later admit he often felt more at home behind bars than on the street. He certainly was not rehabilitated during his imprisonment. Drugs were readily available to him inside the prison, just as they are to the inmates in most prisons. As a mid-1990s examination of Pennsylvania's prison system that included the prison where Tony served his time found:

> Several prisons within the Pennsylvania Department of Corrections (PDC) system were suffering from widespread drug availability and use: Six inmates died of drug overdoses during 1995 and 1996, assaults on corrections officers and inmates had increased, and the press reported corruption among the staff and collusion between inmates and staff in obtaining drugs. (Feucht and Keyser 1999:11)

Consequently, behind bars, shut off from society, and supposedly being either appropriately punished for his crime or at least rehabilitated, Tony, in fact, continued using heroin the entire period that he was incarcerated. He also did not gain any skills for survival on the streets or for seeking legitimate employment once he was "returned to the community." Instead, again like many inmates, he learned from more senior inmates how to be a better criminal. Under the tutelage and protection of his Puerto Rican relatives, he "did his time" without further major infraction of prison rules. He learned to stay under the radar of the prison's administration, keeping a low profile and, to the degree possible, staying out of trouble. When he returned to the streets, he was 22 years old. He had become an adult behind bars, an experience that no doubt had impact on his view of the world and his place in it.

After his release, lacking any alternatives, Tony returned to Philadelphia to live with his father and to again sell dope for him, thus beginning an ongoing revolving-door cycle of crime, imprisonment, release, and rearrest. He was now a seasoned criminal, whose closest friends were criminals, who really knew no other way to live. Nothing in his prison experience taught him a different way or gave him aspirations of conventional success. He did what he knew, what made sense in light of the world as he understood it, the values he had been taught, and the social barriers and opportunities he perceived.

• Chapter 4 •

Becoming a Dope Dealer

Drug selling corner

You know the dealer, the dealer is a man
With the love grass in his hand
Oh but the pusher is a monster
Good God, he's not a natural man
The dealer for a nickel
Lord, will sell you lots of sweet dreams
Ah, but the pusher ruins your body
Lord, he'll leave your, he'll leave your mind to scream
God damn, the pusher
God damn, God damn the pusher
I said God damn, God, God damn the pusher man.

—Steppenwolf, "The Pusher"

Street-level drug dealing appears to be less lucrative than is
generally thought. We estimate the average wage in the
organization to rise from roughly $6 per hour to $11 per
hour over the time period studied. The distribution of
wages, however, is extremely skewed. Gang leaders earn
far more than they could in the legitimate sector, but the
actual street-level dealers appear to earn less than the
minimum wage . . . in spite of the substantial risks
associated with such activities.

—Steven Levitt and Sudhir Alladi Venkatesh,
An Economic Analysis
of a Drug-Selling Gang's Finances

DEMONIZATION

As part of its public campaign to fight drug use, the U.S. Office of National Drug Control Policy (ONDCP) regularly makes and airs prime-time antidrug messages that appear on TV screens across the country. In the aftermath of the tragedy of 9/11, these ads took on a new, more pointed look by asserting that buying drugs funds terrorism. In one of the ads, a young man grimly states, "Yesterday afternoon, I did my laundry, went out for a run, and helped torture someone's dad." In another, a youth reports, "Last weekend I washed my car, hung out with a few friends, and helped murder a family in Colombia." Somberly, the ads conclude, "Drug money helps support terror. Buy drugs and you could be supporting it, too." In the contemporary world, the goal of these ads is clear; if you can link drug use to absolute evil you can prevent the selling, buying, and use of illicit drugs. To support this assertion, $10 million was poured into making the first two 30-second TV ads and print versions that ultimately appeared in nearly 200 newspapers around the country.

The ads are fair, accurate, and justified according to the ONDCP. "Every time you buy drugs, the money goes to people who hurt, kill and maim," explained ONDCP spokesperson Tom Riley. A number of social scientists, drug policy advocates, and drug control experts, however, question the factual accuracy of the ads. "It's despicable and dangerous," argues Ethan Nadelmann, executive director of the Drug Policy Alliance, an education and advocacy group that supports the development of alternatives to the War on Drugs. "When you start labeling tens of millions of Americans as accomplices to terrorists or de facto murderers, you are creating and stirring an atmosphere of intolerance and hate-mongering that ends up being destructive and dangerous to the broader society." Adds Eric Sterling, president of the

Criminal Justice Policy Foundation, "This is an effort to demonize drug users" (Singer 2002:4).

There is grim irony that in the same era neuroscientists were able to use brain scans to show that observable alterations in brain anatomy and biochemistry underlie continued compulsive use of psychotropic drugs and, as a result, the U.S. National Institute on Drug Abuse made the point that drug addiction is thus a "brain disease," U.S. society is witnessing a return to the old practice of equating drug users with evil. Old convictions die hard even in the face of disconfirming facts. Like social policies, strongly held ideas often can withstand the onslaught of facts because their roots lie deep in culturally constituted emotions and bedrock moral understandings about the way the world really is. Facts that don't fit with embedded beliefs can be questioned, disputed, or ignored. Convictions that don't match the facts need not be jettisoned; indeed, cognitive dissonance theory suggests they may be embraced even tighter. Simply put, culture and social interest almost always trump research and findings, at least in the short run (a period that can extend across one or more lifetimes). Ideology fails when its costs so outweigh its benefits that alternatives become credible options.

The roots of drug users' demonization date to the passage of the first federal antidrug laws early in the 20th century. The ultimate social effect of this legislation was to label drug users and dealers as criminals. In the aftermath of this labeling, illicit drug use and sales came to be synonymous with deviance, lack of control, violence, and moral decay. By then, drug addicts—who in previous generations had included noted writers, playwrights, statesmen, and even physicians—had lost all credibility and social standing and had become "pretty much worthless humans in the popular imagination" (Kane and Mason 2001:241). As Goode (1984:218) emphasizes, "by the 1920s the public image of the addict had become that of a criminal, a willful degenerate, a hedonistic thrill-seeker in need of imprisonment and stiff punishment." Indeed, as David Courtwright, Joseph Herman, and Don Des Jarlais (1989:3) remind us, "Some extremists in the 1920s and 1930s even proposed firing squads as a permanent solution for the drug problem, on the theory that the only abstinent addict was a dead one. " Whether depicted as immoral and depraved, in effect, the devil incarnate, or as a naïve handmaiden of modern-day terrorism, drug users and more so drug dealers, came to fill an important role in society, namely that of the bogeyman, the social embodiment of nightmarish evil and unlimited harm. The street drug dealer in particular became the ultimate negative role model, an individual who lived over the edge of conscionable behavior in society and thereby served a useful social function in efforts to limit deviance and narrow the range of acceptable social behavior.

Based on the analysis of an extensive set of interviews conducted with active drug users in New York City, Alisse Waterston vigorously disputes many of the conventional truisms about street drug addicts and dealers and the causes of their behavior. Based on her analysis, she is most critical of the tendency to portray working-class addicts and dealers as if they constituted "distinct and autonomous social phenomena," a world apart (including categorically differentiating drug users and sellers in the streets from those in the suites) (1993:27).

Instead of exoticizing and dehumanizing people who buy and sell illicit drugs on the street, we should attempt to understand the "basic social forces, such as economic activities, class conflict, and labor-market composition" (Waterston 1993:29) that drive their behavioral patterns as well as the web of meanings and beliefs said to be part of the "drug subculture." In other words, demonization, which involves turning real people into dark, unknowable, mythologized entities because of their extreme difference from "people like us"—including seeing low-level drug users and dealers as the ultimate cause of most of our urban problems—stymies our awareness of social inequity as a substantive factor in social unrest, street crime, and drug use itself.

We fail to recognize working-class drug addicts and their street suppliers as casualties rather than causes of urban decay. Instead, we use them as scapegoats, blaming them for why our homes, our streets, our communities, and—with the alleged terror–drug connection—our country are unsafe. In effect, they are individuals trying to cope with the hidden injuries of class, racial, or other structural oppression, and they are worthy of empathy or even understanding, to say nothing of deserving access to effective treatment. The price we pay for our constricted heart and mind is the reemergence, generation after generation, of people like Tony who endure enormous personal costs, while generating significant costs for society as well (through repeated arrests, incarcerations, and inadequate treatment).

BACK IN THE WORLD

Hitting the streets after such a long incarceration during a developmental period when many people acquire the employment skills that will sustain them through much of their lives, Tony faced several major life challenges. He had no money or money-management skills, no job training, no familiarity with how to get or keep legitimate employment, no experience with preparing meals, not to mention how to develop and sustain a romantic relationship. All of these had either been banned, unavailable, or irrelevant in prison. Moreover, since he had never stopped using drugs while incarcerated, he still craved them, indeed, much more so than when he was arrested. By all measures, Tony's probability of returning to illicit activities leading to rearrest and reimprisonment were immense.

In 2004, the U. S. Sentencing Commission released a study of recidivism among first-time criminal offenders. The commission differentiated three types of first-time offenders, of which Tony would have qualified as category one or "true first-time offenders": individuals with no prior arrests or convictions. About one-fifth of individuals in the criminal justice system who, like Tony, fit the category-one definition had a prior history of drug abuse and fewer than 10% used a weapon or engaged in actual violence during their first offense. Nationally, over 60% of all male arrestees test positive for having illicit drugs in their system at the time of their arrest (National Institute of Justice 2000). Recidivism rates among such drug users are especially high; in one study, rates of reincarceration within two years of release increased from 34.8% in 1986 to 44.6% by 1988 (Fabelo and Riechers 1990). An examination of the lives of street drug users and dealers makes it clear why recidivism rates are so high in this population.

Returned to the streets, but now labeled a convict, it is difficult for former inmates to find employment or even housing. In focus group interviews with newly released individuals in an early Hispanic Health Council AIDS prevention study, a common complaint voiced by such individuals was that they were bored and frustrated. Left without much to do, they hang out, as they always have, on the streets, taking in the hustle and bustle of everyday life, meeting old friends, making new ones, trying to find something worth doing, some place worth being. There, they are regularly offered a free "taste" of street drugs by individuals who either are attempting to show their generosity or, more sinisterly, to get someone "hooked" again so as to have another customer for their illicit wares. Recalling such an experience of his own, Piri Thomas writes, "I found my mind thinking, Wonder what it would be like again? Wonder what it would be like again? Wonder what it would be like again? Wonder..." (1967:329). The tumble back into the old life is not far or hard to come by, and happens regularly within a year or two of release from incarceration for many "ex-cons."

Consequently, it is not surprising that upon his release Tony would go back to working for his father, someone he had conflicted attitudes about, someone he ultimately feared and certainly sometimes hated. He really could not think of any other options as he knew little of life outside of what have been called "total institutions." In his classic book, *Asylums. Essays on the Social Situation of Mental Patients and Other Inmates,* Erving Goffman (1961) defined total institutions as involuntary places of residence and work where a large number of individuals, isolated from the wider society, live for a prolonged period of time and lead a structured and formally controlled way of life.

The total character of such institutions is symbolized by the firm barriers that stand between them and the outside world and their constant administration, by a central authority, of most aspects of the inmates' lives. Activities are tightly scheduled, routines are enforced, uniformity of appearance (e.g., uniforms) is required, and the rules emphasize institutional goals, not individual needs. While there is also an informal structure in such institutions that may be outside the control of the formal administration, as will be discussed below, even the unofficial system may impose constraints that require degrees of conformity in inmate behavior. Adaptation to such a way of life, Goffman argues, has consequences for former inmates for life outside of total institutions where, by comparison, individual freedom is great, constant decisions must be made, plans established, and self-supervision rather than supervision by others maintained.

Consequently, Tony went back to his father, where at least he knew what to expect and what he would have to do, and where someone else, ultimately, would still have authority over his life. He stayed with his father for two more years, working the streets, learning the dope peddling trade, and acquiring skills for survival on the streets. During this period, relations between Tony and his father began to change. Tony was now a man and no longer feared his father. In fact, he felt bold enough to try and steal drugs from his father.

> I went for his box, where he kept his heroin. I grabbed it and he caught me. He was chasing me down the street shooting at me. He came close. The bullets were whizzing past my ears. He didn't hit me though. Then we made up a month later and he let me come back to live with him. He forgot about it and said, "You can come back if you want." See, when I was little he would hit me. And after I got out of prison he tried to hit me for something. We started fighting, I didn't hit him hard but he fell back. That is when I realized, he ain't gonna do this no more. He realized he couldn't hit me no more, realized I wasn't a kid any more. He didn't have that power over me like he thought he had. . . . So he picked up the gun. He shot at me but he didn't shoot me.

Having survived prison and already having taken two lives—and having been the recipient of peer respect for being tough—Tony was now confident, even cocky about being able to defend himself in tight situations. Over time, on the street, he also acquired confidence in his ability to be on his own, free of the demands and constraints of others. To make the break with his father, he decided to move back to the only other place he really knew, Parkerton, the Connecticut town he'd lived in during his youth. He even still had friends there from his days with the Omens. Bringing with him a supply of heroin and entrepreneurial dreams of starting up his own drug operation, he headed north.

Tony moved in with his mother and began contacting old friends. Soon, working as a lone operator, he started selling and using drugs. He developed a romantic relationship, rented his own apartment, and, at least temporarily, began leading a relatively stable life, although, as always, one outside the lines of the dominant society.

> I just wanted a change. I wanted to be on my own. But not in a good way, you know. I figured I could bring some stuff [heroin] up [to Connecticut] and eventually go on my own [selling]. . . . Back then I was good. . . . I'm not trying to brag but back then when I needed something I knew how to get it. . . . So I did pretty good 'cause during that time I had a habit but it wasn't [that great]. It wasn't eating into my profit. So I was doing pretty good. I had my own apartment, had a girlfriend that I was taking care of. I didn't have to work [at a legitimate job], everything was being paid on time, bills.

Then as has always been the case for Tony, and for most other street-level drug dealers, things went awry. The streets, as low-level drug dealers learn fast and are reminded often, are intensely dog-eat-dog environments ruled by a sense of limited good and great need. The majority (59%) of the participants involved in drug dealing in the Hispanic Health Council's Drug Monitoring Study, for example, reported that they were homeless and barely getting by. They are pushed, as a result, to take chances, to tempt fate. Dealers try to take advantage of their customers and the latter, in turn, when they can, hustle the dealers.

Drug users live on the edge, a zone in which calling the police seems a preposterous notion because everyone is engaged in illegal activities. But users are driven by intense drug-craving and are therefore always at risk of being "turned" by the police—who know they can tempt most users to inform on the next person up the drug hierarchy in exchange for leniency. Drug users know the rule of thumb is "do unto others before they do unto you." As Ralph Cintron, who studied gangs and drug dealers in a place he called Angels' Town, reported:

> [A]nother acquaintance of mine, the officer in charge of the street-gang task force, had earlier told me about methods of harassment used by the police to keep street gangs and drug dealers off guard. One of the most common methods was to pressure suspects into becoming informers. As the police intensified the suspect's fear of punishment, they simultaneously intensified the suspect's self-centeredness. If the police could get the suspect to put himself or herself first, they had an informer, someone willing to betray others. (1997:158)

Among street drug users, who begin feeling the pain of their addiction if they go too long without finding "the cure" (a common street name for drugs), self-centeredness is unavoidable. Consequently, "[r]ather than experience withdrawal symptoms" brought on by a night in jail on minor or trumped up charges "most addicts . . . will talk" (Hughes 1977:30). As Tony found out when he was robbed by another addict not long after his father first put him on the street selling drugs, drug craving can push a person to dangerous measures. This type of behavior is not unusual on the street. In examination of "war stories" (accounts of street life told by drug users), we found that stories about "ripping off" drug dealers were quite common. For example, one street addict told us:

> "When I say 'do 'em,' I mean I might bring him [a street drug dealer] back here in this back alley and say, 'Give me five dimes' [five bags of drugs]. And when he pulls it out [to sell it to me], I stick him up. I take everything [all the drugs and money] from him. I pull out my pistol and take everything. You stick it right in his face, right in his face. Stick it right in his mouth. 'You know what time it is!' He just give it to you. I tell him, 'You know what time it is.' He got a pistol in his mouth, he gonna give it to me, believe me, he gonna give it to me, happily. I've never had a problem with them. I've

caught [robbed] thousands and thousands, seven, eight, nine thousand [dollars at a time]. [Then you] haul ass. He ain't gonna chase you. Especially when he has to put his clothes back on, 'cause I'm gonna make him pull them down. By the time he gets his pants up and buttoned, I'm out of there, I'm gone! And he doesn't know me from Adam. The only place he might see me again is jail." (Singer et al. 2001:600)

So strong is the ethic of street exploitation that among the stories street drug users tell are tales about the very unusual and miraculous occasions when people treat them with decency rather than see them as potential victims. In our analysis we labeled such stories "tales of uncommon generosity." For example:

"I was up against the corner, and I was sitting on that little bench, the little couch. A guy came up and said, 'Give me everything, your watch, everything.' He had a knife. . . . He had me trapped in the corner. And the way he had me, you know it was like, give it up, and this and that. And see, if I had seen it coming, I would grab . . . you see, I always carry a bottle. . . . I'll crack that over someone's head. They'll think twice about robbing me with a knife or not. . . . I think he was using 'ready' [cocaine]. He probably wanted to get a hit, because I had dope on me and he came in with a girl. And he was like, 'Give me the dope too!' And she was like, 'No, just leave him with the dope. I'll take one bag.' So they left me. I had three bags [of heroin], so they left me with two bags. She took one. He was like, 'Give it all up!' And I was like, 'Yo man, I'm sick, I need it.' And the girl was like, 'No, grab one and leave him with two.'" (Singer et al. 2001:601)

In Tony's case, his incipient drug operation was exposed to the police by a commercial sex worker who was one of his regular customers, very likely in exchange for not being arrested or harassed by the police (Romero-Daza, Weeks, and Singer 1998/1999, 2003). Recalls Tony:

Then I got busted. I got set up by a prostitute. She was a good customer, but she kept asking for too many fronts [i.e., fronting her heroin that she would pay for after turning a trick]. I would give it to her but after awhile, enough is enough; so all of a sudden she set me up. I got busted for narcotics possession and sales of a narcotic substance. I sold it to her. I sold her a bundle, and for some reason they [the police] just pulled up and they had it right there on the table. My stamp [a brand label put on the plastic bag] and everything.

Convicted again, this time on a drug charge, Tony was sent to prison for four and a half more years.

Back behind bars, Tony soon found he was faced with a critical life decision. While prisons are planned, built, and maintained by mainstream society, and ostensibly are run by city, state, federal or private penal administrations, in the cell blocks day-to-day life is strongly influenced if not controlled by gangs. Writing of San Quentin in California, for example, R. Theodore Davidson observes that a Chicano gang called Family, "virtually controls . . . illegal economic activity" throughout the prison, including all sources of money and contraband goods (1978:106). Because the underground economy is critical to the ability of Family members to maintain dignity within the prison, violations of Family authority result in deadly consequences. As a result of constant predation within prisons, Tony like many prisoners was forced to join a prison gang or face the consequences of being on his own without "backup" from fellow gang members. As described in the next chapter in greater detail, he chose a group based in Hartford called Twenty-Love, an affiliation that had impact on Tony's life for many years thereafter. In addition to providing the social support and protection that had been available to him through his step-mother's relatives during his first "bid" in prison, help from Twenty-Love, a drug-dealing gang, enabled Tony to quickly return to dope dealing once he was released.

RUNNING A BLOCK

With new skills learned in jail, Tony now prided himself on his ability to manage a highly profitable and well-organized drug business with supplies provided by his fellow gang members, those with connections with higher-level drug operatives. Following a model he had seen his father use, he set up a local drug distribution site that was staffed by a group of lower-level gang members:

> I was running my block, it was five or six of us. I was vice president [of the gang]. And that means full serve, and there were captains, stuff like that. I tell who what to sell [drugs]. Nobody could sell on that block unless they were Twenties. . . . I had to decide who I could trust and who I couldn't. . . . We used to have one person that stayed at one end of the block and another at the other end, with walkie-talkies. And we'd talk to each other to see who was coming, cops, whatever, and we used signals off of the porch. We would use 5–0 to signal for the police coming [from the TV program, Hawaii 5–0]. . . . I was smart. I know how to run it. Like if you had everybody out there selling dope [heroin], boom, boom boom . . . they get caught. But that is why I had runners, that's why I had guys at the end of the street. I can pay them twenty dollars, 'cause if you try to be greedy and keep all the money for yourself you gonna get caught faster. See, I learned from my father in Philadelphia. He used to have the same thing, guys down at the end of the street looking out, using hand signals. I applied what I learned from him to my business and it worked. . . . I was making about seven Gs [$7,000] a week and paying people. Plus I had the seven [thousand] in my pocket. It was a good business.

As a mark of his success, Tony pointed to his ability to support his girlfriend and their expensive, drug-involved lifestyle without having to work at a nine-to-five job.

Yet drug dealing did not always bring Tony success and reward. Eventually, with each venture in selling drugs Tony would reach a point at which his own addiction would begin to overwhelm "the business." Not only did he "get high on his own supply," also getting high influenced his decision making as a drug dealer. Before long, things would fall apart. One of the worst such examples of this pattern occurred during the period that I was interviewing him. Although heavily addicted, he was able to convince several dealers affiliated with other gangs to give him bags of heroin on consignment, with the idea that the dealers would realize their profit when he sold off the bags at street level, took his share, and turned over the remainder of the net profits to his suppliers. Tony took the consignment of drugs with the full intention of selling them on the street and buying drugs with only his share of the earnings. Instead, the first time he got "dope sick" while trying to sell off the heroin, he used the dealer's drugs in his possession.

> I was selling 50 or 60 bundles a day [worth about $5,000 at the time]. But as my addiction built up, I was getting 50 or 60 bundles a day, but I was only selling 20 and keeping the rest for myself, supporting my habit and my wife's [really, his girlfriend] habit. So I beat [stole from] a lot of individuals for their money and their drugs. I was taking their drugs and their money. They let it go on for awhile because I would come back with a different story. So I would get more drugs, sell it, give them the money, so everything seemed copasetic. Then I would turn around and beat them again. The only ones I didn't beat was Twenty-Love. I really beat the Netas and the Kings. Towards the end, that's when I had to move out of town 'cause they put a contract out on me.

Tony reported that a clear sign that his addiction was out of control at this time was the addition of the tranquilizer Xanax to his drug repertoire. Xanax is a pharmaceutical drug that is commonly diverted for illicit use. It is an example of the wide family of drugs known as hypnotics, substances that cause tranquility, sleepiness, lethargy and stupor, including the tranquilizers, and narcotics (e.g., heroin, morphine). Specifically, Xanax, like Valium, Ativan, and clonazepam is a benzodiazepine tranquilizer that is very effective for treating anxiety. While drug diversion has become a major problem, and pharmaceutical drugs have claimed an increasingly large share of the illicit drug market, the benzodiazepines present an especially grave problem because legal and illicit users of opiates have discovered that the mixing together of benzodiazepines and drugs like heroin (as Tony began to do) or methadone (by methadone patients or illicit users of street methadone) produces a particularly desirable high. As a result, this drug combination has spread rapidly among illicit users.

The better high achieved by mixing these drugs, however, can come at grave cost for the user, including death from drug overdose. In an Australian study, Darke and coworkers (2000), for example, found that 27% of all heroin-related deaths involved co-use of benzodiazepines. In the CDC-funded Drug Monitoring Study at the Hispanic Health Council, we found a strong association between the use of pharmaceutically diverted drugs and participant reports of drug overdose. In the second phase of this study, we found that diverted pharmaceutical drugs like Xanax are widely used among inner-city street drug users, especially among White drug users. Individuals who reported use of a benzodiazepine were significantly more likely than those who did not use these drugs to also report having drug-related overdose experiences (34.6% vs. 21.1%). Methadone treatment programs have been particularly plagued by benzodiazepine use among their patients. Providers of methadone treatment have told me that they hardly have a patient who doesn't know someone who has overdosed on this form of drug mixing. In his own case, Tony reported:

> I was startin' to get heavy into Xanax. I was shootin' up. Plus I was takin' aspirin bottles, emptyin' them out, puttin' water and Xanax, and dope, and sniffin' it while I'm drivin'. I was really bad. I mean I'm bad now but I'm talkin' . . . you know where I was, I didn't even have my right mind with the Xanax. That's why I won't do Xanax no more. It made me . . . blackout. I can't remember things to this day. I see people eat four sticks [Xanax comes in the form of a small bar] at a time with the methadone and they walk around like this every day. They do that every day. I don't know how they function like that. They gotta be in a blackout . . . constant blackout.

CAUGHT

Tony's effort to "beat" his dealer connections worked for quite awhile. However, eventually one of the dealers caught up with him when he left Hartford and went back home to visit his girlfriend in Parkerton.

> When I was walking down the street, waiting for her [his girlfriend] to come back from her trick [commercial sex], I was

going up towards Washington Street. . . . It was ten o'clock at
night. There's like this little alleyway. I take that alleyway
because it's a shortcut, everybody knows that. I used to use it to
hide from the police. That's where they got me. I saw a car go
by and six guys got out. They came out with a blade. They
started to attack me and one dude sliced me like that [lifting
his shirt and revealing a jagged 12-inch slash across his chest
on the left side]. If it had been an inch closer to my heart, I
would have been history.

Violence, of course, was nothing new to Tony. The threat of
violence—emotional and physical—daily preparation for violence
on the street, and enduring the agony of violence-inflicted pain
were all commonplace to him as an integral part of the world of
street drug use and sales. He had come to accept violence as he
had bad weather, harsh but unavoidable. In fact, as discussed
later, the level and diverse kinds of violence endured and initiated
by street addicts and low-level drug dealers like Tony is unsettling.

Once on his own, running a block-level drug ring, Tony came
to take even greater pride in his ingenuity, his toughness, his ability to handle himself on the street, and his capacity to "be a man"
in a violent world. As a "righteous dope fiend," he lived by his
wits and "street smarts," and by the (commonly violated but still
touted) code of the street: "Thou shall not inform to the police"
(Hughes 1977:30). This was his "edge" as he called it. He knew
how to suffer pain with silent dignity when need be and, following
his father's example, was a "stand-up" guy; he kept his mouth
shut, never cooperated with the police, did not "drop a dime" on
others (i.e., give the police information about the illegal activities
of others), even those who had tried to victimize him. Over the
years, he developed a strong self-image as a successful street hustler who knew the ropes and had the attitude and skills needed to
handle himself, as reflected in the following incident:

I was walking down Albany Ave one time by myself at eleven
o'clock at night and a guy pulled a gun on me. But I seen he
had no bullets in there. He pulled it out and he tried to take my
coat and my money, but I looked at him and said "Nah," and
walked away. Then he tried to come at me and I punched him

and knocked him out. See that was stupidity . . . 'cause I don't know if he had any friends but I had to show him that I might be White but I'm not a punk. I was lucky. I take my chances. It's like I knew he wasn't gonna pull the trigger anyway 'cause if you have a gun pointed at someone's head and you're telling him to take off his jacket and give me the money and they don't do it, they start walking away, then you should have pulled the trigger right then and there. It was a chance and I took it, but that's how I've been all my life.

At the same time, during his younger years especially, Tony always felt that "Lady Luck" was on his side, a guardian angel who showed up just in the nick of time when his life was on the line. Once, even, when he was trying to avoid running into a dealer to whom he owed money but had avoided repaying because he had no money to spare, Lady Luck waited cruelly until the very last second before making her welcomed appearance.

I was walking about three o'clock in the morning and it was a fenced area. A car pulls up. It was a silver Cougar. The window comes down on the passenger side and all of a sudden I see a gun. It was a chrome-plated gun. I stopped. I mean, I was scared to death, I had nowhere to run. I was shaking. I mean, I can sit here and say, "Oh I stood up to him and I was talking shit to him. 'Go ahead and shoot me, you can't kill me.'" But, no, I was scared because he had me point blank, dead. I was dead. Almost pissed in my pants, and to tell you the truth, I knew I was dead. All of a sudden the gun clicked. I heard it click, it jammed. When it jammed, I ran and never looked back. By the grace of God the gun jammed.

After he was slashed across his chest, however, Tony's whole demeanor, his regular swagger and soft-spoken bravado, suddenly evaporated. In subsequent interviews, he emphasized the turmoil in his life, his deteriorating health, the growing independence of his girlfriend, and his loss of control over his illicit drug and alcohol habits. He kept turning the stabbing incident around in his head, seeing it as an ominous sign of his diminished capacity and loss of stature.

Before, I just wanted to go out like a trooper. . . . Since the stabbing, I feel like a punk because in my younger days I would have had a gun, a knife. I fought, but not like I would have 10 years ago. That has been tearing at me. Ten years ago, I would have killed somebody. But this thing scared me because I figure I am turning into a punk, you know. I fought back, but I was trying to protect myself more than hurt them. In my younger days I wouldn't have cared if I died or not. I would have killed one of them just to prove my point: don't mess with me! But this time, I was just trying to save myself, just trying to get out of there in one piece. I thought I was a tougher man, but I was just trying to save my life that day. The way I was raised by my father, if you get your ass whipped you keep going back til you whip their ass. Now, it is like "I gotta heal first, you know, and then I might or I might not go back." In my younger days, I would have healed up just enough and took a gun and killed one of them if I seen them on the street.

EVERYDAY VIOLENCE

As Tony's tale in this and the previous chapter suggests, violence on the streets is routine, often harsh, but business as usual. The logic of violence on the street rests on the acceptance of "a kind of brute cause-and-effect relationship in which the humiliation of someone call[s] for an equivalent humiliation of the offender. Its ethos [i]s 'an eye for an eye, a tooth for a tooth,'" a life orientation that carries "a mythic, destructive clarity" that quickly sweeps away ambiguity and allows a rapid, clear response (Cintron 1997:151). Underlying this ethic and the logic of street violence are four assumptions: "life is tough; most people are not to be trusted; always be wary; and defend yourself or get beaten up" (Cintron 1997:154). At times, when the local homicide rate soars, the streets of the inner city begin to feel like a war zone ruled by these toxic assumptions about social life and social others.

In the Hispanic Health Council study in which I first got to know Tony, we interviewed a sample of 224 street drug users, individuals who, like Tony, used drugs daily, tended to hang out on the streets looking for opportunities to hustle money, buy drugs, and slip into an abandoned building or other secluded locale and get high (Singer 1996). When the opportunity arose, many also participated in drug sales, as a look out, runner, or "steerer" (directing people from the suburbs where to go to purchase illicit drugs). We identified a wide range of types of exposure to violence among study participants. Like Tony, who has witnessed a number of his friends and relatives fall victim to violence, 74% of the participants in our study reported witnessing fighting in the streets of their neighborhood during the last four months (Romero-Daza et al. 1998/1999). Violence in the streets was said to be especially common by participants, with "once or twice a week" being the median frequency. Gang violence (reported by 45% of participants), robbery and muggings (42%), and beatings or stabbing (31%) were the most common types of street violence participants reported they had witnessed (Romero-Daza et al. 1998/1999). As one participant stated, "I used to sell drugs [and] this guy killed this woman in the alleyway behind my door and I seen it happen and, you know, I was scared."

Most participants also reported that they were directly involved—as either victim or perpetrator—in additional violence. Thirty-nine percent said that they had been the victim of violence over the past four months, while 30% reported being a perpetrator of some form of violence against others. Specific rates of violence victimization affirm that exposure to violence is not a distant phenomenon in the lives of street drug users. Fourteen percent reported being the targets of physical violence during the last four months, while 7% indicated they had suffered serious physical violence during this period. Significantly, nine of the individuals in our sample responded that they had been the target of attempted murder, Tony being one of them. Moreover, 10% admitted committing acts of violence, while two respondents stated that they had attempted to murder someone during the last four-month period.

Tellingly, of the incidents of violence victimization reported by participants, 71% of physical violence involved the use of drugs or alcohol. In the case of incidents of serious physical violence, the rate of substance use rose to 75%. In cases where study participants reported being the perpetrator, the use of drugs or alcohol was 80% for acts of physical violence against another person, and 100% in cases of serious physical violence and attempted deadly acts of violence. Significantly, 44% of our participants felt that involvement in violence (as either victim or perpetrator) contributed to increases in their rates of drug consumption.

Tony fell into this latter group. After his chest was slashed, instead of seeking revenge, he turned to drugs and alcohol. He began drinking heavily for the first time in his life, and his heroin habit increased from a steady three bags a day when I first interviewed him to eight bags a day. Shortly thereafter, he began regularly smoking crack cocaine as well. For the first time, realizing that things were spiraling out of control—a state that self-help programs like Alcoholics Anonymous and Narcotics Anonymous call "hitting bottom"—he decided to seek drug treatment. While treatment did help him to "lower his habit" (allowing him to use a lower dosage of drugs per day to feel "normal"), he was not able to stop using illicit drugs.

This is not an uncommon pattern among drug addicts and is the reason addiction has been described as a chronic, relapsing disease. The difficulties in overcoming drug addiction, even with the help of treatment, have led some people to the misperception that treatment for addiction is not effective. Existing research, however, shows that addiction is quite treatable, especially if the treatment is long lasting, well delivered, and tailored to meet the needs of the individual patient (NIDA 1999). Rates of success in drug treatment are comparable to those for other chronic diseases such as diabetes, hypertension, and asthma. These increasingly widespread—but unlike drug addiction hardly dishonoring—diseases in the U.S. or elsewhere may, no less than drug addiction, be distressing societal symptoms of contemporary lifestyles and life experiences. While treatment for these chronic diseases does not help every sufferer, adequate and appropriate treatment that addresses the whole person in social context can be quite effective. So too with treatment for drug addiction.

• Chapter 5 •

Into Ganglife

Hartford Correctional Facility

A great deal of gang research has been concerned primarily with explaining the deviant and delinquent behavior of gang members. . . . From listening to [gang] members . . . describe and explain their participation in the gang, it became clear to me that they do not perceive this behavior as an act of deviance or failure. This is not to suggest that these youngsters do not know that what they're doing is against conventional norms of the larger society. . . . They are of the opinion, however, that the gang represents the only course of action still available to them and with which they can challenge existing constraints in and domination by mainstream society.

—Felix Padilla, The Gang as an American Enterprise

At this late date it is disturbing that so many people can read about [gangs], live near, and do research on these longstanding phenomena without noticing that they do not fit the theories.

—Joan Moore, Homeboys—Gangs, Drugs, and Prison in the Barrios of Los Angeles

EXPLAINING GANGS

Much has been written about gangs, and much has been disputed about them too. In book form, this literature began with Jacob Riis' *The Children of the Poor*, Emory Bogardus' *The City Boy and His Problems*, and Frederik Thrasher's influential *The Gang*, which was based on a study of over 1,000 gangs in Chicago, published in 1892, 1926, and 1927 respectively. Early assessments viewed the appearance of youthful street gangs as a consequence of the outlawing of child labor, and the subsequent social emergence of the developmental phase that came to be known as adolescence, a liminal and transitional period between childhood and adulthood. The term adolescent was not coined until 1904 because, before then, large numbers of youth, primarily from the poor and working classes, labored like adults on farms, in factories, and in cottage industries. Compulsory education gave adolescents a place to go but did not accord them much status in society. Rather, like children, adolescents were seen as less than adults and thus were protected more or less from exploitation but were not accorded a meaningful purpose in society or a satisfying sense of self-identity. The result was alienation, which early (and later) theorists concluded was the driving motivation for forming and joining gangs.

The massive waves of immigrants, people with different languages, customs, and values, that landed on America's shores around the turn of the 20th century and afterward, further contributed to the alienation hypothesis. Youth gangs sprung up among the new immigrant groups, as one segregated ethnic enclave after the other (Irish, Jewish, Italian) filled with hopeful arrivals from new places soon discovered that the American melting pot was on a very low flame and opportunities were blocked (Cloward and Ohlin 1960). Discrimination and bigotry, and out-

right threats and acts of exploitive violence, propelled the formation of defensive gangs committed to "protecting the
neighborhood" from the outsiders who sought to prey upon them.
Herbert Asbury (1928), who studied the immigrant gangs early in
the 20th century, wrote graphic descriptions of groups like the
Pug Uglies, the Roach Guards, and the Dead Rabbits (featured in
Martin Scorsese's movie, based on Asbury's study, called *Gangs of
New York*). Asbury recognized that gangs are generally composed
of neighborhood branches that keep together youth who grew up
together, a pattern we have seen again and again in Hispanic
Health Council research in Hartford.

After World War II, the "foreignness theme" (Moore
1978:48) was replaced by the "minority theme" in public accounts
of the composition of street gangs. In his book *Vampires, Dragons,
and Egyptian Gangs: Youth Gangs in Postwar New York*, Eric
Schneider (1999) explores this transition. The initial movement of
Puerto Ricans and African Americans into White neighborhoods
sometimes sparked violent clashes, as captured in the enduring
Broadway hit and movie *West Side Story* and the far less successful
play by singer/composer Paul Simon called *The Capeman*. Despite
this conflict, casualties were limited because, unlike contemporary
gangs with well-stocked hardware arsenals, few of the older gangs
had repeat-fire weapons. Moreover, Schneider asserts, gangs
sought to minimize fatalities by imposing behavior codes (such as
respecting neutral territory and not targeting non-gang members),
an insight that challenges pathological interpretation of gang
behavior. Similar restraints on the level of violence perpetuated
by gangs have even been found among contemporary groups, who
commonly are described as being far more violent than their pre-
decessors (Curtis and Hamid 1999).

The Violent Gang, penned by Lewis Yablonsky (1962), was one
of the first books to espouse the pathological view of gangs. Building on the earlier work of Frederick Thrasher, Yablonsky asserted
that there were three different types of gangs: social gangs, delinquent gangs, and violent gangs, with the latter, although having
limited cohesion, presenting the gravest threat to society. Violent
gangs, he asserted, meet the psychologically pathological needs of

especially troubled youth (one of the explanations for gang involvement satirized in the song "Gee Officer Krupke" from *West Side Story*). Gangs are commonly headed, he maintains, by youth with leadership ability but who suffer from significant psychological impairments. By contrast, Francine Garcia-Hallcom (2000) contends that inappropriately broad definitions of gangs inflate the violent threat of gangs. Many youth who commit violent acts, she points out, have only very loose associations with gangs, perhaps through a family member, and their violence is not really gang related. Others point out that even violence by gang members is not necessarily gang-organized violence, but rather may be the actions of individuals who happen to have a gang affiliation.

Alternately, according to Walter Miller (1958), culture—particularly working-class subculture—is the source of gang delinquency. He argued that six values are especially emphasized among blue-collar families, namely a belief in fate, valorizing autonomy, appreciation of toughness and "smartness" (sometimes called "street smarts"), desire for excitement, and trouble seeking, and provide the generating milieu for gangs and their antisocial behavior.

As we have seen in chapter 2, the parents of gang members and their faulty socialization practices, their failure to serve as good role models, and their alleged unwillingness to provide adequate supervision of their offspring are other common motifs in discussions of the causes of gang formation and affiliation. In his later work, Yablonsky (2000), for example, has argued that children who grow up in abusive or otherwise dysfunctional homes, including those where the parents abuse drugs, tend to have low self-esteem and are significantly more likely to participate in gang violence than other youth. In Riis' words from over 100 years ago, "inordinate vanity . . . is the slum's counterfeit of self-esteem" (1892:237). Chemically dependent parents, Yablonsky further argues, lack the ability to teach their children how to be caring and compassionate and compassionless youth make violent gang members.

Gangs often have been seen through a moral lens. Although public moral panics about the threat of gangs to mainstream society come and go, gangs in one form or another remain, but not necessarily the same form. The edginess of such panics increases as gangs grow in size and scope and begin to take on the language and symbolism of quasi-independent nations (e.g., the Black Stone Nation, the Almighty Latin King Nation) and self-proclaimed rulers of inner-city terrain. Panics surge when gang members are exposed as controllers of large illicit enterprises, like drug production and distribution systems, gun sales operations, or large-scale carjacking rings, as gang members are connected to violence against non-gang members, and gangs show signs of spreading beyond individual neighborhoods or cities through the development of branches in multiple locations.

One location that has caused considerable public concern is the prison, which has become a fertile spawning ground of new gangs. As Moore (1978) showed in her study of Chicano gangs, continuities and affiliations between prison gangs and street gangs are strong because of significant parallels in the day-to-day experiences of gang members. What Moore did not find, however, was that defective personalities or dysfunctional families were primary sources of gang affiliation. She did not find great homogeneity among gangs, arguing that a stereotype has formed that blocks understanding of variation in gang organization and behavior. Because of the stereotype, the assumption is made that "A gang is a gang, is a gang" (Moore 1993:28).

Felix Padilla who, like Richard Cloward and Lloyd Ohlin, saw gang formation as a response to blocked opportunity, describes the Chicago Puerto Rican gang he studied not in pathological or deviance terms but as an ethnic enterprise: "a distinctive entrepreneurial strategy historically developed and used by immigrants and their descendents in response to their marginal economic position" (1992:3). Like Tony's block-level drug business described in the previous chapter, illicit substances—which cannot be sold by legitimate businesses—represent an ideal commodity for a group blocked from economic success though conventional channels.

Support for the enterprise model comes from available information on a Hartford-based gang with which Tony had an affiliation and drug-selling relationship called Los Solidos (The Solids,

meaning Those Who Can be Counted On). Los Solidos formed
in Connecticut's prisons during the early 1990s when the remnants of two other gangs merged in an effort to protect themselves from predation from larger gangs like the Latin Kings.
Following unification, Los Solidos became a formidable force in
prison and on the street and quickly attracted a new generation
of younger members who found that the gang offered opportunities to make money as well as provided a strong sense of family-
like group solidarity.

Los Solidos quickly became a major player in the local heroin
trade. To consolidate its organization, Los Solidos developed a formal group structure that included several key roles, such as godfa-
ther, president, vice president, and enforcer, and implemented a
ruling "committee" composed of the top eight to ten most powerful members in the gang. The Los Solidos rulebook, which fell
into the hands of the police with the arrest of group members, dic-
tated that "the committee" is the heart of the gang and that any
judgments or decisions it makes must be respected by group members (Singer and Mirhej 2004). Part of the power of the Committee lay in the fact that it alone had the authority to activate the
"enforcers" to handle group problems (usually by intimidation or
outright physical violence).

In the mid-1990s, *Harper's Magazine* acquired and published
Los Solidos' rulebook. Reflecting the group's business approach,
the manual included a set of formal instructions for members who
worked in the "laboratory." While mention of the specific product
manufactured in the laboratory is carefully avoided, it is evident
from numerous arrests of group members that it was used to
divide bulk heroin into individual bags for street sales.

Gang members themselves, especially ex-gang members, have
tended to emphasize gang affiliation as a search for respect. Isis
Sapp-Grant (2000), who was once a member of the New York
girls' gang, the Deceptinettes, and who left ganglife and became a
social worker who counsels youth at risk for gang involvement,
argues that she and her friends joined the gang because it offered
a sense of power and respect, experiences that were not otherwise
available to her in society.

Finding a similar pattern among young Latino crack dealers, Bourgois (1995) titled his study *In Search of Respect*. He argues, "One message the crack dealers communicated clearly to me is that they are not driven solely by simple economic exigency. Like most humans on earth, in addition to material subsistence, they are also searching for dignity and fulfillment." 50 Cent, the popular hip-hop singer and former crack dealer, has said the same about his own illicit life on the street. Commonly, in our own studies at the Hispanic Health Council, youth have justified their acts of violence by saying they were "disrespected" by their victim. Concludes Vigil:

> Basically, the street gang is an outcome of marginalization, that is, the relegation of certain persons or groups to the fringes of society, where social and economic conditions result in powerlessness. This process occurs on multiple levels as a product of pressures and forces in play over a long period of time. The phrase "multiple marginalization" reflects the complexities and persistence of these forces. (2002:7)

What does Tony's individual case tell us about the various theories of gangs described above? This issue will be examined in the remainder of this chapter but especially in the one to follow after it. It is clear that there are different kinds of gangs in different places at different points in time. Realizing this, gang researchers have tried to develop typologies of gang organization and activity. As a moral panic over gang activity begins to recede, however, and the level of research on gangs subsides, efforts to explain gangs narrow and interest wanes, only to be replaced a decade or so later by a new wave of interest.

An enduring insight, however, is that we have not solved the challenge of how to provide realistic opportunities and decent lives to the working class during periods of sharp economic transformation and upheaval when old opportunities collapse and old sources of human respect and dignity are shattered. Instead, the working class has been treated as a dispensable group that must adjust on its own to shifts in the economy. If so, it can be expected that gangs will continue to be one of the agonizing social costs of such an approach to change.

FINDING LOVE

After his initial flirtation with ganglife as a preteen member of the Omens, Tony's return to gang affiliation, as noted in the last chapter, occurred following his second arrest while incarcerated in a Connecticut prison.

> When I came back to Connecticut, I got arrested again, for selling drugs. I went to Sumners Prison. While I was there I joined the gang Twenty-Love [a predominantly African American street gang]. At that time there were not many White members, maybe 20 or 30.

Although like many prisons across the country there was a White supremacist gang in the prison, Tony avoided having anything to do with them.

> There were the BOWS, Brothers of White Supremacy. They were an offshoot from the Aryan Nation, but they had their own people. You see the spiderwebs [tattoos] on their elbows. A couple of Hartford cops are ex-BOWS. You could see the spiderwebs and they're either Aryan or BOWS. There was a big thing about one cop in Hartford . . . he has to wear elbow patches to cover the spiderwebs 'cause that's an Aryan symbol. But I grew up mostly in the projects with Blacks, Whites, and Puerto Ricans. . . . So I felt comfortable with Blacks and Puerto Ricans. I wasn't comfortable with White people sayin' "nigger this," "nigger that." I didn't feel comfortable with that . . . I didn't feel comfortable with the Aryan Nation 'cause they're always, you know . . . even though they had the meth [methamphetamine] coming in [to the prison], I just didn't feel comfortable with them kinda people. And I guess they didn't like me either 'cause I used to hang with Puerto Ricans and Blacks.

Although he had had drug buying connections already on the street with the two smaller groups who would eventually merge to form Los Solidos, he decided to join another gang in prison, a larger group that was gaining strength and that was aligned with the Los Solidos in their conflict with the Latin Kings. Regarding his decision to join Twenty-Love while in prison, Tony explained:

If you were solo [in prison] you get your stuff taken away. Like if you had a brand new pair of sneakers or boots or something, it always ended up like that. Somebody gonna steal from you if you're not down with anybody. And, I [had] connections already, see. I [had] connections with the Solids [Los Solidos]. . . . If I needed [drugs or] if something happened to me, they would help me out, or I would help myself out. . . . [In prison] I affiliated with Twenty-Love. Back then it was the Magnificent Twenties. . . . In jail and on the streets, Solidos and Twenty-Love are cousins. They watch each other's back. . . . To tell you the truth, with the families [street gangs] in jail now its. . . . better than trying to be on your own. 'Cause, instead of one-on-one, you're gonna come full force [i.e., have fellow gang soldiers to watch your back and protect your interests]. You know you have to prove yourself sometimes. They tell you to do this and if you do it, you're in. You got no problem [with other inmates]. You know, it depends on what they tell you to do. If you gotta stab somebody, you stab 'em. 'Cause in the long run you're gonna get stabbed if you don't do it, so you might as well do it. They just told me to do it. I had no problems with him [the victim] or nothin'. I just had to do it. 'Cause if I didn't do it, I knew I would have been next. That's the thing you gotta deal with in there. It's a different world.

Tony soon found his niche within Twenty-Love as a gang enforcer.

I became an enforcer. The enforcer is in case anyone needs to get done or terminated, eliminated. I was the one. Either you're doing it or organizing it. . . . We had to terminate one individual. We came at him with five guys. We got him in the corridor. He was taken to the hospital by helicopter. He didn't survive. As the enforcer, I did what had to be done. If you do something to someone and he survives . . . he's gonna come get you. Beat downs [a punitive assault or rite of passage beating], that's what I did. I know we beat down three people that was part of us [fellow gang members]. They didn't come back with the money [owed to the gang] they were supposed to. But I didn't get charged with that. Nobody got charged. It was . . . people kickin' him, stompin'. It was a bloody mess. And then just left for dead.

They scooped him up, aired him outta there [taken by helicopter to an emergency hospital]. When you're inside, you can't
have a heart, you can't have feelings. You just gotta do it, you
know what I mean. 'Cause if you have a heart, you're not goin'
to survive. When you're in there, number one is yourself . . . and
whoever your partner is at the time . . . or your clique, 'cause
they're watching your back and you're watching theirs. Twice I
was even the target of beat downs because I turned on a couple
of my brothers 'cause I thought they were disrespecting me. I did
not like to be disrespected so I shanked [stabbed] two of them,
didn't kill them. I stabbed one in the neck and one in the kidney. Instead of being terminated for this, the gang, knowing the
type of individual I was at the time, I just got a beat down, a
two-minute beat down. No facial shots 'cause they don't want
the CO [correction officer] to know but they give body shots,
your legs, everything. You get two minutes but they gotta hit you
as hard as they can. I got hit in the kidneys and I had to go to
the hospital in prison, 'cause they bruised one of my kidneys
bad. For a whole week I couldn't move, I was very sore and black
and blue. You can't fight back, you just take the beat down.

Beyond his involvement in clandestine gang activities in
prison, Tony spent much his time in prison reading, watching TV,
and, when possible, getting high.

You can go to the library. You can get a book. You can read. You
can watch TV. I mean, prison . . . I mean, as they say, "prison is
where your mind is." I like to read. I read a book. I read the
paper. I read a magazine. I do something. I'll draw. I even went
to classes and got my GED in prison. But if you sit there and
just let your time go slow . . . you're gonna be bored and you're
gonna go stir crazy. [And] we were selling dope and 'caine
[cocaine] in our [cell] block. We either had the COs who were
down [i.e., were gang members themselves] . . . see, there's a
lot of COs would be with the Latin Kings, Solids, Twenty-Love,
and even the BOWS. Either them or even have people come in
on visits, if they're on your visit, they bring it in.

Tony also added, "I never got sexually assaulted. I never had
sexual relations with a man in prison."

As Tony has discovered again and again throughout his life, it is far easier to get drugs than drug treatment, even in prison. While Tony found friends and a gang affiliation in prison, he did not find what he most needed: effective drug treatment or job training.

> They had AA meetings for coffee and donuts. Then they stopped bringing donuts. There is no rehabilitation. They say there is but there's none.

Instead, while incarcerated he struggled to keep his drug use under control. The goal was not recovery from addiction, rather it was using drugs when possible while maintaining only a low-level addiction.

> I controlled it because you didn't want to catch a bad habit; you didn't want to eat up your supply because it didn't come in [to the prison] on a regular basis.

A TRIP TO THE ISLAND

After prison, Tony hit the streets again, and resumed his risky life pattern, running his block selling and using drugs. Then, he was arrested once more.

> I got arrested for assault on a paramedic and a police officer. We had been drinking on the corner, me and friends, and someone dropped acid [LSD] into my bottle. I knew it, that was my choice. I got so obliviated [sic], drunk and all messed up. I went on a rampage. Driving into cars, crashing. Then the police stopped me and I started fighting with them. I broke a paramedic's jaw and a policeman's nose. I got charged with driving while intoxicated, reckless endangerment, assault, and risk of injury. I was out of control.

As a result he was returned to the penitentiary for several more years, picking up his life behind bars where he had left it with his fellow members of Twenty-Love. Following his release from prison, Tony left Connecticut and went to New York, where his father was now living and still dealing drugs. Once again, continuing his zigzag life pattern, he began working for his father, which quickly produced the same results as before. He was arrested for possession of drugs and sentenced to do time, initially on Rikers Island and later at Attica. Rikers, which actually holds 10 different penal facilities (nine for men, one for women), is the main jail for New York City and is located on a 4.5-acre island in the East River. Most prisoners housed there—usually 15,000–18,000—are either serving short sentences, awaiting trial (and hence not even convicted of a crime) or sentencing, or about to be transferred to an upstate facility. The island was named after Abraham Rycken, a Dutch settler who farmed the island, but it was converted into a prison facility in the 1930s after being acquired by the city.

Prisoners at Rikers still joke about a painting that was donated to them by Salvador Dali when he was unable to keep an appointment to speak at the facility. The painting hung in an area that housed prisoners for several years until it was moved to the lobby for safekeeping. In 2003, the painting was stolen (and replaced by a fake) and has never been recovered. Ironically, three guards were found guilty of the theft. Attica Correctional Facility is a common destination for prisoners transferred from Rikers. Infamous since the prison rebellion of 1971 that left 40 people dead, it is memorialized in the song "Remember Rockefeller at Attica" by famed jazz musician Charlie Mingus.

When Tony was sentenced to go to Rikers, his uncle immediately informed him that a relative of the man he had killed in Philadelphia was imprisoned in Rikers and had vowed to get revenge against Tony. Once again, Tony was in a position to have to defend himself in prison or face painful consequences.

> When I got out of prison in Connecticut, I went to New York. I didn't have to make parole, I did all my time. I don't like making parole 'cause I get in trouble [once out on the street, leading to parole violations and increased prison sentences]. But I came to New York with my father and my uncle. I don't know what happened but I got caught right away with half a stack [of heroin] 'cause I was bringin' it to my father. Somehow it seemed like I got set up, I don't know. So I had to go to Rikers and that's why I had to go and do that guy, 'cause Rikers is wide open. That's

why I was scared. For the first time in my life being in jail, being in Rikers Island, was scary. Because I was White, I was scared. If it wasn't for my uncle knowing this Puerto Rican man, I would have been killed there a long time ago. But what happened was, that guy, that guy I killed, his family was there . . . one of them. And he tried to do me but the Puerto Ricans and the Italians, they used to hang together in Rikers. . . . They gave me the go-ahead, so my uncle told me I had to do this guy before he did me . . . 'cause, you know, we wanna end this thing he told me. I didn't kill him, I just got him in the kidney. He had to get transferred. But I had to get him or else it wouldn't end. But when I did that, it seemed like I got respect from the rest of the dudes in there . . . 'cause a lot of White dudes won't fight back in Rikers Island. Rikers Island is crazy. They got swords in there like this . . . you know, like a foot long, two feet long . . . actual swords. They're like in the blocks like crazy, hidden in chinks in the wall. . . . I did four years but not all in Rikers. I did two years in Attica. Attica is just like you see in the movies . . . rapes, lotta rapes, lotta fights, lotta murders. I seen a lot of people die up there. Attica is a wide-open penitentiary. If you don't fight back or do what you gotta do, you'd be raped. Connecticut's prisons are nothing like prisons in New York.

By this point, Tony was familiar enough with prison life to know how to get by. As has been his pattern, he kept his head low, kept himself busy, and did his time. Unlike some prisoners, he did not watch the clock, did not count the days. Such behavior, he had learned, was not the way to survive incarceration.

MEN OF TOMORROW

After his release from prison at age 28 (after his first drug dealing arrest), Tony returned "to the community" to live in a housing project near to his mother's home in Connecticut. He continued to hold a positive view of gangs and to serve as an enforcer.

I went right back to my block. Everyone I knew was there. Back out on the street, I was a vice president and an enforcer

for Twenty-Love. I would execute targets. Say if one of my
brothers was in a beef with a member of a different gang, he
might go to the gang [Twenty-Love] and talk to them and ask
that that other guy get a beat down. We would carry it out ourselves. Sometimes it involved drive bys [shootings].

During this period, Tony helped to turn the remnants of his
old gang, the Omens, into a local affiliate of Twenty-Love. In a
burst of self-confidence, the group took a new name: Men of
Tomorrow (MOT). Within this larger group, which eventually
grew to about 35 members, Tony developed a small set of close
personal friendships, indeed the only friendships besides romantic
relationships that he ever talked about during our interviews. As
is common within the embedded hierarchical structure of many
street gangs, this closely knit "clique" or crew of six individuals
regularly socialized and engaged in gang-related money-making
activities together as a unit.

Well, in the projects, in the gang, it was like brothers, family.
You know, especially for me, it was more close. The brothers
were more closer to me than my family was. Back then there
was like the MOTs. We had 35 guys, but you know, there would
be cliques of like who you really hang with, so I usually had like
five or six other guys that I really was close with. You know,
we'd be together all the time, go drinking, go out, go to the
bars, start trouble. We were always together, these six guys and
me. You know, so it was like family. That's what we called them,
family, brothers. So, um, what's the word? Confident, something like that. You could go out to a bar, and, you know, the
way you walk is swagger, you know, look at somebody because,
you know, you had four other guys backing you up. So you were
out to really cause menace, you know, when you're young like
that. That's what it was about.

In addition, he continued to maintain his relations with the
two other gangs (Savage Nomads and Ghetto Brothers) he had
known while in prison, which would come together as Los Solidos. Before long, the MOT developed hostile relationships with
several local gangs.

We used to come up to Hartford when they had the Italian Fest
[a street fair in the local Italian community on the south end of
Hartford]. And we used to hang with the Ghetto Brothers,
Savage Nomads, [and] cause trouble there, big fight, rumbles. I
think that's what really ended the Italian Fest . . . all the
fightin' and all that. Yeah, 'cause out-of-towners would come in
and start fightin'. So I think that's really why they put a end to
it. [W]e had the Savage Nomads and the Ghetto Brothers . . .
come down [from Hartford] and hang with us. You know I met
Benny Gonzales [a Savage Nomad leader] before he died and
all that. A lot of guys from Hartford I know from way back,
they would come down to the [local] carnival; we would all
hang together. And the Earles and the Drifters would come
and stay on their side of the carnival, and at the end of the
night we'd rumble.

Many street gangs first coalesce as social groups engaged in
recreational activities and only later acquire the outlaw attitude
and illicit activities that leads others, including local law enforcement, to define them as a gang. The Diamonds, the Latino street
gang from Chicago studied by Padilla (1992:93), for example,
began "as a musical group, playing their music on street corners in
their neighborhood and in local neighborhood nightclubs" and
only converted into a vengeance-seeking street gang when one of
the members was killed by a gang member from another neighborhood. Often, even after they have become a full-fledged gang, with
covert illicit operations and a history of "gangbanging" (fighting
with rivals), such groups will publicly deny they are a gang and
claim that their only function is to serve the community by spon-
soring parties, dances, and other leisure activities. While MOT was
clearly a gang, deeply involved in drug sales and other illegal activities, regular socializing and having fun was an important feature of
ganglife. Built into some of these activities was a commitment to
taking care of and providing services for the local community.

I mean we used to have humongous parties in the project. I
mean, cookouts, everybody was invited from the projects. We
used to have . . . at the housing authority office, they had this
one big, huge wall. So we rented a projector and we used to

have movies every Friday night for the kids. For our kids, for
their kids, for the whole projects' kids. We used to do it every
Friday night during the summer. [W]e'd kick up dues. We'd
have our dues. You know, you pay five dollars a week . . . stealin' to raise money for the keg [of beer]. We have a keg every
night . . . two kegs, two dollars a person. You know, and then
we'd have summer parties at the beach and we'd take over . . . I
remember we used to go down to Old Lyme [a shore town in
Connecticut, where Lyme disease was first identified], and
there used to be a rest stop. Everybody would be at the beach
but our party would be at the rest stop and have big huge . . .
make, uh, lemonade, ice tea punches, you know, liquors.
Women would come, girls, we had our groupies, you know you
sleep with one. Everybody slept with you know, there would be
five girls that everybody slept with, gang bangs and all that.

Not surprisingly, as defined by gang members, "fun" tended to
include behaviors condemned by mainstream society, including
stealing, to provision group parties, and feuding with opposed gangs.

[W]e used to hang in the park, across the street. . . . And then
right here would be the package store [i.e., a liquor store]. So
every time the beer truck came he would load up [his hand
truck], you know, [and] go into the store, [and] five [MOT
members] would run down there and grab five cases, come
back out. He'd be on the other side of the truck, [we'd] grab
five more of the 32-ounce-bottle-of-beer cases. So by the end
of his thing we'd have about maybe 25 cases of 32-ounce beers.
We used to love when the beer trucks come. Liquor, we used to
grab a case now and then, but that was harder. Stealing cars,
joy riding through the park. We used to have a party at the
park every night. And then the Earles or the Lords would come
at the end and start fightin' with us. It always ended in a fight.
Somebody got stabbed, beat up bad. Back then it was a lot of
hand-to-hand fightin', or knives. It wasn't guns like it is now.
We weren't quick to kill anybody, we just wanted to fight, or
hand-to-hand, you know, one-on-one. Sometimes it would
start out as a one-on-one and then, BOOM, the whole circle
would just beat up, you know. All the time it ended up like that

though. One-on-one and then BOOM, everybody's fightin' or
jumpin' in. But that was fun for us. That was every night.

Although described by Tony as fun—reflecting his valuing of
always being tough, on-guard, and ready to "throw down"—inter-
group conflict often involved heinous violence.

I broke my hand three times [in street fights]. . . . But I mostly
stabbed a lot of people or cut people. Chains. I remember I
took, um . . . , we were at Don's Place, it was a bar, we used to
hang there. One day the Drifters, one of them got hurt so then
they all came down with their motorcycles and they tried to
come through the door like they were gonna do something. But
we had bottles set up. We just started throwin' 'em at 'em. They
came there with chains. I took one chain away from the guy, he
tried to get on his bike and I clipped him right from here to
here [indicating from one side of his head to the other], split
his head right open from ear to ear. I seen him like a week later,
he told me he had 36 stitches. Sat down at the bar and chatted
with him. That's how it was.

In such conflicts, neighborhood acquaintance could supersede
the structurally encouraged local ethnic tensions that have long
served to keep the working class internally divided and disorganized.

One day, this biker followed us home into the projects. He was
drunk and he wanted to fight one of our brothers. So our
brother came out there with a golf club. He started beatin' him
in the head. I came running out of my house, started beatin'
him in the head with a golf club too. And then all kinds of bik-
ers came and then all of a sudden the Blacks and the Puerto
Ricans started helping us and BOOM, BOOM, you know,
there was a big rumble in the projects.

Through such shared experiences, the Men of Tomorrow
evolved a multiethnic membership, which differentiated them
from other groups.

White, Black, Puerto Rican, whoever was in the project
[joined]. We were all project kids and basically . . . that's why
the other [local] gangs . . . at that time, the Earles, the Lords,

the Drifters, they really didn't like us 'cause we were mixed. We used to hang around the Cobras . . . and the Cobras were Puerto Rican. And then Savage Nomads and the Ghetto Brothers from Hartford used to come to our project and party with us when we had big parties.

Despite their hostilities, gangs would socialize at neutral sites, like certain bars, that were located in no-man's zones between the turf areas claimed by local gangs. At such locations, fighting was forbidden—a rule groups would (usually) follow because, apparently, there were benefits to interacting with rivals, including the collecting of information and the opportunity to meet girls attached to other gangs.

Then we used to go to The Celtic, that's a bar. All the Earles, the Lords, everybody would meet there 'cause Johnny McGarry [the owner] was a Westie. He was an Irish guy from New York. So he made sure it was a neutral place. Nobody could fight there and if you did, you was dealt with. But one night I was really messed up on dope and everything and I was drunk. He had a nice oak door, you know, one of them big doors that would swing open that was nice and carved. And his first day he put it on, I was drunk and they kicked me out of the bar 'cause I went into the bar that night and I had a starter pistol [a gun used to start races] and it was a joke. One of my brothers that was in my crew, he was dancing on the dance floor. But I had the starter pistol, nobody knew it was a starter pistol, only me. And I was drunk out of my mind. I went out to the dance floor, took the gun out pointed it at his head and I said "you tried to get my girl." It was a joke. Oh man. Everybody scattered in the whole bar, people were ducking down. It was a joke. So the bosses grabbed me. So I punched one bouncer and then the guy I pointed the gun at pounced on the other bouncer and chairs were flying, women were flying, everything was going. And they finally grabbed me by the neck and this is in Johnny's bar . . . Johnny's dead now but, um . . . so the boss and these four guys are throwin' me out the door so I kicked the door on the way out and this is a solid oak door. Somehow my foot went through it. I guess when you're that high and drunk and your adrenaline is going, you get a little stronger than you usually are. I put a hole in the door. So I had to get my father [to come up from Philadelphia] to sit down with Johnny, 'cause he was like, I was barred for life. And you know, all the guys are there on Thursday, Friday, and Saturday and I can't go in, you know. So I had to pay for the door and my father had to come in and smooth things out, 'cause Johnny actually wanted to have me killed. So my father had to come and talk to him and all that to smooth things out 'cause he really wanted me dead. I mean, plus I broke the windows on his Corvette that night.

Not all fighting, however, was with rival gangs, "town/gown" tensions were another source of conflict, reflecting underlying class tensions and resentments between the emergent middle class and the working class from which the former were, but one generation (and a college education at state university) removed.

And then we used to go to this bar, um, it used to be down the street from [the local state university], you know, we were going there with our colors on, you know leather vests, wore black vests, and motifs, you know. The college kids, you know, they'd be snotty, you know, "what does that mean?" We'd say, "Men of Tomorrow," and then somebody would say something stupid. It would either be the football or the wrestling team. I fought a wrestler bigger than me and he was crazy. He kept looking at me, you know. And I was just there, you know, I was tryin' to pick up this girl. She was very beautiful, you know, a college girl and I wanted to be with her. But he kept looking at me, staring at me. I said, "Listen man, you got a problem?" He goes, "Yeah!" I said, "What's your problem?" He said "You're my problem. All you guys are my problem." Right. He said, "That's our girl. She's in our school. She don't need no thugs tryin' to pick her up." And she wanted to be with me. He says, "If you're man enough, you can come outside." So I look at my friends, you know, my brothers and they said, "Just let it go." 'Cause there were a lot of cops that could . . . you know, a college bar. We would be the ones arrested anyway. And then he pushed me. I said, "Okay, it's time to go outside." But he let me go around the corner of the building first. So I was waitin' and I said, "I'm waitin.'" . . . He comes 'round the corner, I take his head and I bang it against the brick, blood started going every-where. But I give him credit though. He was still trying to get me in like a wrestling headlock and all that, and he had me on the ground. So I had to put my fingers in his eyes and start squeezing 'em, just to get out of this headlock, that's how good of a headlock he had me in. His way of fighting was wrestling like they do in the wrestling matches. I mean, he was trying to choke me. So the only way I can get out of it was to put my fin-gers in his eyes and start trying to push his eyeballs out. And that worked. And then the cops came and I got arrested for assault. He got me in the headlock, me, and they see it . . . [but I got arrested] because he was bleeding and had a concussion. Little things like that was normal for us.

Normal, of course, is culturally defined. Even for Tony, the gangbanger's life would, over time, come to appear far less appeal-ing than it did in his youth.

Chapter 6

Out of Ganglife

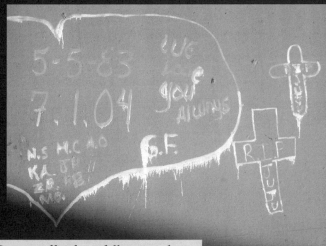

Gang graffiti for a fallen member

Just as defining a gang and establishing criteria for membership are problematic, determining when and whether membership has ended also is difficult. Does it mean, for example, the termination of relationships with gang members? Or alternately, does leaving the gang mean the cessation of illegal activities associated with the gang, such as selling drugs or participating in gang fights?

—Scott Decker and Barrik Van Winkle, Life in the Gang

No one wakes up one day and decides to become a doper— especially a street junkie.

—Alisse Waterston, Street Addicts in the Political Economy

GRAVE CONSEQUENCE

In his youth, Tony saw gang feuds and fighting as expected, commonplace, largely unremarkable, as well as good material for morning-after tales to share with peers who missed a particular fight. Still, he knew such behavior was not without grave conse-quence, including, over time, the death of all but one other mem-ber (ironically, according to Tony, one of the toughest guys in the group, who eventually left ganglife and became a minister) of his personal clique, losses that weighed heavily on Tony and troubled him for many years. They probably trouble him even now.

When Gary, a member of my crew got killed, I went berserk again at The Celtic. The way it was, he went there [to the bar] with Peppy. Peppy used to be in the Dukes, right? Gary was a drunk but he would never back down from a fight, but he couldn't fight that night, he was so drunk. He couldn't even stand up. So the guy had a gun, right? . . . pulled it out on Gary. Gary took his knife out, but Gary couldn't even stand straight. So the guy took Gary's knife and stabbed him in the heart, and Peppy was right there and Peppy didn't do nothing. And when I got there and I seen him, I went berserk. And I seen Johnny kind of laughing so I took a swing at him and knocked him out. And I was barred, for life, again. But I didn't care at that point. I really wanted to burn that bar down because . . . Johnny had a beef with me so I think he put this guy up to this [stabbing Gary]. 'Cause the guy wasn't drunk and he knew Gary was drunk. But he went to jail, and we had one of our brothers in jail and he [the man who stabbed Gary] didn't get killed but he got beat up bad. They had to move him to the New Hampshire prison 'cause he was gettin' death threats and all that and he was gettin' beat up every time they seen him. Not just by one of our brothers, but friends [participated] because that's what

101

being with a lot of people like us, like the Ghetto Brothers and Savage Nomads. So they had to move the guy to New Hampshire. And he only got seven years, for murder.

Then another one of our brothers got shot. He was walking through the plaza and ran into these two guys came back from Marines. Ike was black, and these guys were in the Marines and they didn't like niggers and all of the sudden they had a rifle, and for the hell of it they just shot him, just to shoot somebody. And it happened to be Ike walking through the plaza, twelve o'clock at night. And the military took them away. And then Bugsy got murdered by one of the Lords. They shot him up with brake fluid. They got him in jail, he got murdered in jail.

After Gary, Bugsy, and Ike were murdered, another member of Tony's clique, Peppy, committed suicide. Tony suspected that Peppy felt responsible for Gary's death and was overwhelmed with guilt feelings. Additionally, Tony knew that Peppy was struggling with understanding his sexual identity as well as with other problems. More recently, Marty, a fourth member of the clique, also died; again drugs were involved.

Peppy killed himself with Xanax and Valiums and liquor [three central nervous system depressants] and wrote a note, said he just couldn't take it anymore. This is right after Gary died. . . . Peppy just couldn't take it anymore, he said. And he had girl problems. And Peppy was like, he didn't know his sexuality. He didn't know if he was gay or straight, you know what I mean. He was having a lot of mental issues and he just took himself out. Marty died recently, in 2003. He was in Desert Storm. He came back Post Traumatic Stress Syndrome and all that. He wasn't the same. He wasn't a heroin addict when he went, and he came back out—he was a heroin addict. The thing was that one of our brothers, from, you know, the past . . . we all kept in touch, you know. That's gang kid stuff there but when you grow up you're still hanging. One of the things was, a guy gave Marty some drugs from New York. Real potent dope and Marty was doing Xanax and I guess he OD'd because five days later, five days later . . . I mean his was a little apartment complex and when I walked into the hallway, I could smell the body. I

found him. And I don't understand how these people . . . I
found him five days later but these people are walking in-out of
the hallway and smellin' this stench of death and not saying
anything. I kicked the door in and he'd been dead for five, six
days. If you've ever seen a body dead five, six days, it's not a
pretty thing. I still can't get Marty out of my head and that
night I found him. Seeing the way he died, you know. I just . . .
it kind of freaked me out.

ILLICIT ENTERPRISE

Within the broader framework of partying, which among
other functions likely serves as a release from the tensions of
intergang hostilities and violent feuding with parallel gangs from
surrounding neighborhoods, as well as from anxiety about regularly risking imprisonment, a central component of ganglife was
illicit enterprise. For a group like the Diamonds studied by Padilla,
the turn from a focus on turf battles and retaliative violence targeted at enemy gangs to profit making involved a shift from buying marijuana in bulk for distribution and use among group
members to selling it on the street to an ever-widening array of
customers. Soon, Padilla notes, "Money-making through drug
dealing came to represent the gang's emerging chief function"
(1992:54). Part of this transition involved the adoption of a "busi-
nesslike character" in the organization of gang affairs. In the case
of the Men of Tomorrow, gang business had several key compo-
nents, especially selling.

> Weed, cocaine. Of course me, I was sellin' dope. A lot of acid
> [LSD], a lot of hash [hashish, a potent marijuana derivative].
> We got the, um, we got a lot of narcotics. Or whatever we can
> get our hands on.

Other regular illicit money-making activities involved the
theft and resale of merchandise from local businesses.

> My six guys, we would go out and make our own money too,
> stealing cars, whatever. Go to stores, steal steaks. I mean, not

just one or two packages. We would go to every store around
that area . . . and get like thousands of dollars worth of meat
and have a cookout or sell it. We used to sell a lot to bars. Try to
break into pharmacies, [we] broke into three pharmacies. . . .
There was a blizzard, I forgot what year it was, um, Kendo [a
member of Tony's wider circle of 35 gang members] had two
snowmobiles. . . . So what we did, we knew it was coming on
the news. So we took a wagon, we took the wheels off, tied it to
the snowmobiles. . . . The package store was down the street
from the project. Both snowmobiles with the wagons on it
busted through the window and took all the liquor we can get,
loaded it up, and the cops couldn't even catch us. That's what
kind of stuff we used to do in the area, in the neighborhood.

For a short period, Tony even tried legitimate employment;
although, because of his deep involvement with drugs, this didn't
work out very well. Seeing that his coworkers at the hospital
where he had found employment were also using drugs, he quickly
reverted to the job he knew best.

I worked at the hospital as a cook, you know. My uncle was the
head cook there so I got a job there, but drugs was a part of my
life. I was sellin' pills to the workers—dope, cocaine . . . anything they wanted. I sold it to them . . . even guns.

After this brief and unsuccessful fling with mainstream
employment, Tony quickly returned to drug dealing, among other
illicit endeavors. Through his gang connections, he began to
acquire quantities of drugs in Hartford for street sale back home
in Parkerton. His source was Luigi's Bar on the south side of Hartford, a popular drinking spot owned by a member of the New
England Crime Family headed by Raymond Patriarca of Providence, Rhode Island.

When he was just 17, Patriarca was arrested for the first time
and convicted of breaking alcohol prohibition laws in Connecticut.
By the time he was 30, he had been arrested four more times on
various charges including breaking and entering, "White slavery"
(a term that stems from the turn of the 20th century when there
was a widespread panic that young, middle-class women were at

risk of being kidnapped and forced into becoming prostitutes), and organizing a jailbreak during which a guard and a trustee were killed. During his life, Patriarca was arrested or indicted 28 times and served 11 years in prison. By the mid-1950s, he had risen to the head of the Boston branch of the Mafia, which controlled Connecticut rackets as well. Patriarca soon moved his crime empire to Providence and appointed an underboss to run Boston. Patriarca oversaw an array of illicit operations across New England, including gambling, loansharking, pornography distribution, truck hijacking, and drug trafficking. Drug distribution was handled by a set of freelance operators who paid Patriarca a fee to do business. One such operator was the owner of Luigi's, a site used for loansharking, illegal gambling, and fencing stolen goods.

> We were coming to Hartford to cop the cocaine. . . . We were getting a lot of it from Luigi's Bar. They were part of the mob [Mafia]. Luigi's was out of Boston. Boston and Rhode Island used to be the mobsters [that] ran Hartford. You know what I mean? I used to sell Luigi guns. You know, anything hot, he would buy, especially guns. I'd go to the back table and I'd lay them there . . . naturally unloaded. I was getting guns from New York. Clean guns, no serial numbers, no nothing. Nobody on it [i.e., not associated with past crimes]. You know, my father actually turned me on to one of the guys that he knows, a friend of his [who sold guns illicitly]. You know, sometimes I would go to Brooklyn to get the guns. But I used get cocaine from New York too. My father turned me on to one of his friends there for that too. But Marty [who was a relative of the owner] used to go to Luigi's bar a lot [to buy drugs].

> And on the north end of Hartford on Homestead Avenue there was a guy, a black guy, big dealer also. Today, even the stores, the *bodegas* [mom and pop stores in the Latino community], they're selling. You can get drugs inside the store. Right there on Watson St. That Dominican store. He sells a lot. And in the North End it was . . . even back in the nineties when I remember there used to be a store there on Albany Avenue. I used to go in there and buy half a stack, all the time, every day. And come out with rice and beans and half a stack of dope or

cocaine. There is important stores and bars in Hartford. They still do it. It's not just McDonald's [where heroin is sold by a local Latin King gang member and diverted pharmaceutical pills are sold by several local pill pushers].

With his closest friends dying, Tony turned increasingly to drugs for solace. As his level of addiction went up, and he began to need ever-larger quantities of heroin to achieve the same numbing effects that he craved, he began to turn on his suppliers. Taking 50 bundles on consignment, he would sell 20 and inject the rest. As he put it:

> I went from drug dealer to big-time drug user. I didn't have no more car and I started stealing again. Selling anything. Hustle this, hustle that. . . . Someone said, try this, hit the rock [crack cocaine]. Man, I hit that rock. I was on a roll with that. You want to talk about progressing down, I even went down worse on that. I run into some inmates [guys he knew from prison] and we started doing a lot of returns. We started going to stores, boosting [shoplifting], returning [bringing the stolen merchandise back for a refund], or selling [pawning the stolen merchandise], boosting, returning again. Doing a lot of returns. We didn't do many Bradlies Stores [department stores], but one day I got arrested four times at four different Bradlies. My friends said not to do it, but I was so sick, I would say let's stop here and I ran in to the store. I got busted the first time; they took me to jail and I got PTA [promise to appear in court without bail]. Went to another store, got popped there and again I got PTA. They didn't catch the earlier arrest in their records. I never went to the court dates, and I got failure to appear [in court] and went back to jail for two years on that.

While he was still on the streets, to cover his loses with the dealers, Tony invented elaborate stories and was able, for a while, to get away with it. Dealers know addicts. They know they lie, and often lie well. Lying is a survival strategy for them; conning people is a well-honed and respected skill. Even the dealers fell for his lies about what had happened to their product. But the clock was ticking. The lies were piling up. The money they were owed was not coming back. Tony had been a good salesman, productive; he had made them a lot of money. For a while they cut him some slack. But drug dealers are not known for their patience when it comes to getting their money. Eventually one of the dealers put out a contract on him. News of it reached Tony through the grapevine. He knew immediately that he was in dire straits. To avoid being killed, he fled town.

Tony moved up to Hartford and lived in the shadows. But he grew restless and lonely, and after awhile, thinking that perhaps things had cooled down, he decided to visit his girlfriend. It was during a visit back to his hometown that the dealer finally caught up with him and inflicted the chest wound described in the last chapter. Thus ended Tony's turbulent career as a drug dealer. But there was little else he knew how to do.

After Tony got out of jail for the fourth time, he even considered going back to selling drugs. He would pleasantly recall how he used to make a lot of money selling the little bags of heroin, the sense of success that came with feeling his pockets fill with crinkled dollar bills. The memory served as both a burden and a pathway back to better times. Times before AIDS, before things seemed to spiral out of control in his life. Unable to find full-time employment, he roamed the streets hustling. Frequently he was asked by a local drug dealer whom he knew from the old days to begin selling drugs again. It was an offer he found hard to resist. It was only his fear of being sent back to prison that kept him from going back to the drug trade.

> I am afraid to go back to jail. I'm too old. Jail isn't summer camp no more. It used to be. Jail is jail now. You go in there, it's not fun. . . . I've seen dudes get thrown over the railing at Sumners [a Connecticut prison]. I've seen dudes get stuck in the neck and a helicopter had to take them to the hospital. I've seen one guy get stabbed to death.

THE SAME THING OVER AND OVER

Concerns about going back to jail helped motivate Tony to stop using drugs in 1997. The following year, in his mid-30s, he made a decision to leave Twenty-Love. At the time, he was trying to help his girlfriend (who he often referred to as his wife) get her children back from the Department of Child and Family Services. They shared dreams of quitting drugs and living a more conventional lifestyle.

> I went to the gang and told them, and they gave me a "walk out," it's like a beat down. They understood what I was trying to do and they respected that. I was still affiliated but as an OG [old gangster]. I didn't have to be an enforcer, I didn't have to do nothing, but they could come to me for advice.

At the same time, he began to seek legitimate employment, but his past haunted him.

> I went today to the state. I went for help. They say, "But you're able to work," and I say, "Yeah I'm able to work. I want to work, but it's getting harder and harder to find a job with my record. I need help right now, I need a place to stay for my wife and my kids." Stuff like that, that's when you turn around and you want to sell it [heroin] to make six hundred dollars a day because you actually see what the state is doing. I see who's getting state [welfare] money and who's working. When I ask for help, it's not available; so where else do I turn but the things that I know? I fill out job applications, but as soon as they get to that one thing at the bottom: have you ever been convicted of a crime? Sometimes I put yes, sometimes I put no on it. When I put no, I get hired but two weeks later I get fired [because of background checks]. If I put yes, they say well we don't have nothing. 'Cause everyone think you come out and try to do the right thing, you try, but the right thing to you is not possible if no one's gonna give you a helping hand or let you do it; it doesn't work. So many guys I know right now, they're so frustrated right now with the system. We're trying to get a job, a legit job. But how can we get it 'cause when we get to that question and they look at you. . . . I don't know, I'm tryin' my damndest right now. Sometimes I wish I was back in jail. I don't want to go back for something stupid, but seems to me I'm more adaptable to institutions. I can do better. I can cope better.

Unfortunately, because of these frustrations, and the self-medicating system he had embraced many years before, his attempt at a conventional lifestyle was short-lived. After awhile, he dealt with his problems in the usual way. After six months of being clean, the longest period of sobriety since his teen years, he fell back into using drugs again.

> It seems like every time something either goes right . . . , it could be the sunniest day in the world . . . it could be everything going right . . . being lucky . . . and, I don't have to have anything wrong in my life to go back to it [heroin]. If I'm clean . . . say that time I was clean for six months, when I went back to it nothing was wrong. There was nothing going wrong. Everything was going right. I was doing what I was supposed to be doing, so called, what this world says is normal; I was doing it. But I just went back to it. It seemed like I wanted to get high. I missed it, like I needed it. I was wondering if I could do it like I do in jail, once a week. Can I do it? It would be nice to get high once a week, especially something you love so much in your life. And once I did it once, the next day, the next day and the next day then you catch a habit.
>
> When [people] take opiates [the first time], it takes them a little bit longer to catch a habit, you know, 'cause they never did it. That's why doctors won't give them prescriptions longer than a month, whatever. But if I stay away maybe a month and [then] if I do it two or three days in a row, my habit is right back. It's mentally and then physically [it] comes back. Once I get like a stomach twinge, then I know I'm hooked again. And maybe it's mentally at that point and I could've just stopped, but I choose not to. And the people around me. That doesn't help either. It seems like everyone you know [is using drugs]. I go to NA [Narcotics Anonymous] meetings and all that, and it is true what they say; stay away from people, places, and things [associated with drugs]. But it seems like all I need is somebody from the past, and that's it. And I don't know if I will ever be clean. That scares me too. It seems like I'm never gonna accomplish anything in this life. That scares me. I go from jail to the shelter [halfway house]. Then one time I had a car, I had

my own place, and I go right back to the shelter, jail, street. It just seems like I keep doing the same thing over and over.

Despite his fear of further incarceration, Tony realized that in some ways

jail is much easier. I'm gonna put it this way, it's like I'm taken care of. I don't have to worry about anything and I could just do what I want . . . to a point. I know I'm institutionalized . . . that's what it seems like though. I don't have no responsibilities.

On the street, life continued to be harsh, threatening, and filled with land mines. Not surprisingly, despite his best efforts and strong desire to stay out of jail, before long, Tony was back behind bars. This time the charge was assault in the first degree.

They changed it from attempted murder to first-degree assault because it was in a bar . . . [and] the guy, he knew me from prison. He thought I did something to him but I never did anything and it wasn't me. He came at [me] with a gun. He tried to shoot me. I grabbed the gun and his friend stabbed me here [pointing to his side] and I stabbed him. So I got first-degree assault. And then they tried to give me the gun charge because they say the gun was mine, but it was his so they put us both in jail. The gun had a body on it [had been used previously in a murder], so it was first-degree assault. But it was the other guy's gun, not mine. We were put in different prisons 'cause he was trying to murder me. And then I tried to kill him too, actually, to be honest [during the fight].

For his latest arrest, Tony served a year and a half in prison, during which his mother died. His memories of her, conflicted and remorseful, stay with him always, both in his heart and etched on his arm where there is a tattoo of a large red rose with the word "Mom." From the prison, Tony was transferred for six months to a halfway house, which found him a job in the community. But he had to return to the house immediately after work each evening. While at the half-way house, he slipped back into his "prison drug routine."

I never had like a habit like I have on the outside because it costs more unless you have somebody bring it in to you. I had

somebody but then I lost her. She went to jail. So I was buying
it maybe once a week, I would snort a bag here or there. Or if I
got lucky, I got a syringe.

Upon his release from the halfway house and the constraint of
a curfew, he quickly returned to a full-blown addiction within a
few weeks.

I've been out . . . two weeks, going on three weeks out here and
I'm back again [using drugs]. It didn't take much. I started up
[using drugs] there actually, in the halfway house. Heroin.
Shooting cocaine, the works.

Getting older and formally out of the gang's day-to-day
affairs, Tony still lived as he always had, but with less verve, less
success, less sense of adventure. He lacked the support and structure the gang or even prison had given him; he was at loose ends
with himself. Mostly he felt that he was too old to be a gangster
and too young to die.

LESSONS IN LIVES

As we have seen, researchers, social commentators, policy
makers, moviemakers and playwrights, lyricists, the criminal justice system, and the general public have all developed different
understandings of gangs and why young people join them and
through them engage in illegal and often violent behaviors. While
no single life can provide answers to all of the questions that have
been raised about gangs over the last 80-odd years of gang discourse, Tony's life is nonetheless suggestive.

In assessing the theories presented at the outset of this chapter,
it does not appear mental illness accounts for Tony's behavior. Like
most addicts, he suffers bouts of anxiety and depression, without
question, but, then so do millions of people, young and old, who
never turn to gangs or drugs. Certainly, Tony's family was an influencing factor in his road to gang affiliation, including both his
father who modeled drug use and gang affiliation up close and personal for Tony as he was growing up, but also his mother, who

sternly rejected him because he was a daily reminder of her errant ex-husband and proved it with his wild behavior, which was more than she could handle alone. Equally important, however, were the economic challenges faced by Tony's mother after the divorce, when she was forced to be out of the home working multiple jobs and thus to leave Tony in the ineffective supervision of his sister, thereby opening the door wide for him to turn to the always alluring and adventurous streets. It was there in what is sometimes referred to as a midget gang, the Omens, that Tony found the friends, acceptance, and excitement that were not to be found in school. As a working-class boy who lacked much family support for completing high school, Tony made the choice many inner-city kids make. He picked a street education over book learning. As the case of his sister shows, this was not the only course open to him.

No doubt being sent to live with his crime- and drug-involved father and similarly engaged paternal and step-relatives, which led ultimately to the beginning of drug addiction and involvement in drug dealing, followed by seven years of "prison education" in how to be a better outlaw, helped to cement the life course Tony has followed since the age of nine or ten. Significantly, for a number of years, Tony was a successful gang member and drug dealer. Gang-affiliated drug dealing, in fact, helped Tony to address his underlying feeling of insecurity and low self-esteem. He grew proud of his skill as a drug dealer and his prowess as a man, as he and the subculture he participated in defined that role. Certainly, Tony's approach to drug dealing was a business model of entrepreneurial endeavor.

While at a very low level in the larger, regional, national, and global drug trade, he was an active and, in his own eyes, at times quite a successful operative in the world of illicit drug capitalism. In short, Tony's case would suggest the utility of a *multilevel macro-micro structural model of gang involvement* (as depicted in the figure on the following page). Such a model exhibits important linkages between (1) the wider political economy of class and ethnic relations, (2) various local context and historic factors, and (3) the life experiences and subcultures developed within socially imposed ethnic and working-class enclaves in poorer sections of cities (and in even-less-urbanized areas, as gangs are no longer only found in cities), including the (4) gender roles and life patterns of working-class families. Additionally, the model considers the role drugs play at (5) the individual level in self-medicating the injuries of discrimination and the frustrations associated with blocked opportunity structures, and at the social level as a mechanism for resistance to subordination through the initiation of outlaw enterprises that offer (to some and for some period of time, at least) alternative routes of success. Finally, at its lowest tier, the model incorporates an understanding of the individual as an active agent confronting life's challenges and opportunities as they are presented to him/her in terms of one's location in the larger social hierarchy and set of meanings offered by the mainstream cultural and subcultural systems. This is the type of model that has been developed by critical medical anthropology to understand the social realities behind "disease," including addiction (Baer, Singer, and Susser 2003; Singer et al. 1992).

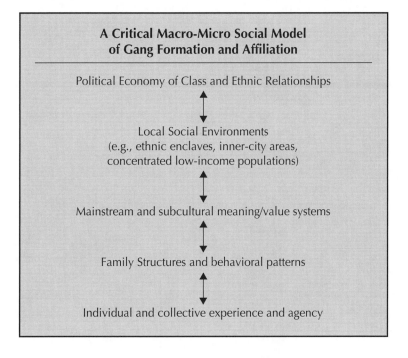

**A Critical Macro-Micro Social Model
of Gang Formation and Affiliation**

Political Economy of Class and Ethnic Relationships

Local Social Environments
(e.g., ethnic enclaves, inner-city areas,
concentrated low-income populations)

Mainstream and subcultural meaning/value systems

Family Structures and behavioral patterns

Individual and collective experience and agency

Chapter 7

Drugs and Romance in the Time of AIDS

AIDS mural

*The unexpected emergence of AIDS in the early 1980s
seemed to reverse the historic trends of the twentieth
century. It signaled the return of the industrialized nations
to what we had assumed was a vanished world of
epidemic disease. . . . In the United States, epidemic disease
soon provided an image of catastrophe that supplanted
nuclear war in terms of media attention, academic
scholarship, and individual preoccupation.*

—Shirley Lindenbaum, "The Making of an Epidemic"

*Today, patterns of social organization and life-styles of
cultural subgroups that have previously gone unnoticed or
unremarked have, in the evolving of AIDS, assumed a new
significance. . . . Nowhere has this been more evident than
in the case of the transmission of HIV through
sexual contact and drug injection.*

—Manuel Carbollo and Giovanni Rezza, "AIDS, Drug
Misuse and the Global Crisis"

I WANT TO LIVE

On the morning of August 12, 2000, the people of Milwaukee, Wisconsin, opened their newspapers to find a front-page article describing a sudden rash of deaths among local drug users. During the previous two weeks, eight drug users in the surrounding county had died, all because of drug overdoses with very pure South American heroin. This significant spike in drug user deaths was not unique to Milwaukee. Similar jumps have been reported along both coasts and in inland cities. For the year 2000, for example, Yang (2001) reported 300 heroin overdose fatalities for just the city of Baltimore, a known center of heroin consumption nationally. During 2001 and 2002, the Cook County, Illinois, medical examiner recorded 628 deaths—six a week—from heroin and other opiate overdoses (Bebow 2004). Nationally, overdose fatalities rose about 50% in 1990–1997, from 10,000 to 16,000. The Centers for Disease Control and Prevention reported that between 1990 and 1997, the drug-induced death rate per 100,000 population was 5.6. For males this figure was 8.4 compared to 3.6 among females (Sporer 1999).

Notably, smaller cities in the country had a disproportionate share of this increase. Thus, while overdose fatalities dropped by 50% in New York City in 1988–1997, in Kansas City there was a 1,300% increase. For example, in Project COPE, a National Institute of Drug Abuse-funded study of AIDS risk and prevention among injection drug users (IDUs), our research team at the Hispanic Health Council and colleagues from the Institute for Community Research began tracking a cohort of street IDUs during the period 1992–1994. In all, we completed four waves of data collection with this cohort. Of the 1,275 participants enrolled in the project, 5.5% had died of various causes, ranging from drug overdose to HIV infection, by the year 2000. Calculated in terms of

117

deaths per 100,000 population, this represents a mortality rate that is at least double that of the general population of Hartford (ages 15–65). Given the number of cases we were unable to find for follow-up interviews, it may be that the rate is higher still in that many may not have been found at follow-up because they had died.

Overall, White drug users have experienced a more dramatic jump in overdose fatalities compared to their African American and Latino counterparts. Drug users who are over 35 years of age experienced a rise of 65% in drug overdose deaths and the rate among those below 35 years of age declined slightly (Coffin 2000). Research by Copeland and colleagues (2004), in fact, found that prior to the emergence of the AIDS epidemic, drug overdose was the principal cause of death among active drug users. While tobacco use remains the single leading drug-related cause of death in the United States and is responsible for half a million deaths each year, as the mortality statistics for illicit drug users suggest, this population has an exceedingly high rate of death as well.

Overdoses have been linked to a number of factors, including periodic changes in the purity of drugs sold on the street; the mixing of several different drugs together, especially those that have a depressant effect on bodily systems; and release from prison or other transitions that move addicts from contexts in which they have had to cut back their level of use because drugs are comparatively scarce to contexts in which drugs are again much more abundant and available (and users proceed to use drugs at their old dosage levels for which they longer have tolerance).

Some drug users have reported to our research team that there are drug dealers who intentionally spike their drugs with dangerous substances that make people sick. Drug users tend to flock to street brands of heroin that have been associated with drug overdoses, on the assumption that such brands must be the most powerful on the street at the moment. These users are not aware or choose not to be aware of the fact that the substance added to the drug to increase its level of potency can have fatal effects. Often those who purchase these drugs believe that those who previously overdosed did so out of ignorance of their tolerance level and that overdosing can be avoided.

Still, it cannot be assumed that all drug user overdoses are accidental. Drug users, especially those who are not new to illicit drug consumption, generally are familiar with their tolerance levels for the drugs they use and consciously seek to avoid overdosing. Consumption of drugs in quantities that exceed these levels may represent attempts to commit suicide, which, as the 11th leading cause of death in the United States, is more common than is generally recognized. In a study of 78 drug users who were hospitalized with nonfatal drug overdoses, for example, Neale (2000) found that almost half reported suicidal thoughts or feeling prior to their overdose. In our interviews with drug users at the Hispanic Health Council we periodically interview individuals who report trying to kill themselves through planned drug overdose.

In 1998, after he was cut on the chest in the retaliatory attack for not repaying the dealer the money he owed, Tony almost joined the ranks of drug users who have intentionally used their drug of choice to commit suicide. He reported:

> Two weeks ago I tried to kill myself. . . . I didn't care if I lived or died. . . . It's about I really don't care anymore. I took a bundle and a half of dope and 14 Xannies (Xanax). You know what, I walked into the Emergency Room, by myself. I told them what I did. I'm still here. I don't understand. What's he [God] want? It's like I'm living on the edge. I'm doing what I'm doing living actually day by day. I wouldn't care about dying, but now I have this fear of death. I never had the sight of death before. I never cared. I'm afraid of dying now. I don't want to die like this [addicted, depressed, and alone, living in a homeless shelter]. This life is gettin' to me. Before I used to enjoy it. Believe it or not, I used to enjoy living like this . . . hustlin' . . . doin' all this. It was, you know, exciting. Now it's to the point where I'm waiting just for it to end, you know.

In Tony's case, depression had become an increasingly significant factor in his life prior to his suicide attempt. Ultimately, he was admitted to the psychiatric ward of a local hospital.

> After being in the nut ward for a week, they put me on Zoloft [an antidepressant medication]. I don't even know what that

is. It hasn't done anything for me yet. I've seen the commercial.
They said I have an anger issue, too, in the nut ward. I'm more
angry at myself because I know what the right thing to be doing
is because I've tasted it one time but I . . . I don't know why I
can't do it. Why don't I like responsibility? A lot of stuff [mem-
ories] are coming back from my life that I've done in the past
and I don't understand why it's coming back right now. It's
scaring the hell out of me. Like that time when I killed that
individual when I was younger, that's coming back. You know,
his family used to write me letters every week [saying] you
killed my son, murderer, and I used to sit there and read them.
I paid for that . . . but yet that's coming back in my life today
and I don't know why. I don't know what triggered it all. I seen
a movie about victims' families and this family [in the movie]
did the same thing [write letters to him in prison]. Maybe that's
why it is coming back, seeing that movie. And a lot of other
stuff is coming back. My father whipping me, stuff like that. I
mean, I'll sit here and cry, I don't know why, and when I do I
just want to get high worse. Somebody was telling me that I
might have traumatic stress, whatever. Sometimes at the weird-
est times, stuff will pop in [to my mind] and that's what scares
me. Actually, I think I'm trying to get a conscience. The scary
part is losing your edge, lose your edge out here [and you are
vulnerable]. I'm starting to lose my edge. If I start to have a
conscience out here, or if I feel bad for something that I do
wrong, that's gonna cause me to go to jail, or have me dead, or
make me go crazy. Lately things are starting to do that.

Fueling Tony's depression as well is the knowledge that he has
AIDS, among other life-threatening diseases.

HIV/AIDS

Acquired Immunodeficiency Syndrome (AIDS) can claim
title to being one of the most devastating diseases in human history. Caused by a contagious retrovirus known as the Human
Immunodeficiency Virus (HIV), the disease has spread rapidly to
all to human populations worldwide. The global count of people

living with HIV/AIDS infection reached 40 million by the end of 2004; millions more had already succumbed to the disease. Although HIV/AIDS is now found everywhere, it is not equally distributed among the populations and subpopulations of the world. Rates of infection are especially elevated among illicit drug using populations.

Since the epidemic began in the early 1980s, injection drug use is believed to have been the cause of more than one-third (36%) of AIDS cases in the United States. From 1998 to 2002, an estimated 240,268 AIDS diagnoses were due directly to injection drug use, with males accounting for roughly 72% of these cases (CDC 2002). In recent years, there has been a gradual decline in the number of new AIDS cases in the United States that are directly associated with injection drug use, but this route of infection remains a prominent factor in the U.S. AIDS epidemic, and an increasingly significant factor in the epidemic globally. Ironically, during the era of AIDS, injection drug use has been spreading around the world at an alarming rate.

The appeal of injecting, explains Tony, is the "rush" that comes so quickly with putting heroin or other powerful psychotropic drugs directly into a vein.

> The rush you get from injecting, it's a trip. It binds you up. It's just overpowering and you feel it from here [pointing to his head] to your toes. In your stomach, if you're sick when you get that first rush in the morning, everything flips. Your stomach isn't turning no more. It just flips. Your body starts getting that warm fuzziness, that's what I enjoy. Ain't nothing like it.

Originally, it was thought that the direct sharing of syringes was the sole reason so many IDUs were developing HIV/AIDS disease. Many thought the symbolic and ritualized syringe-sharing experience helped drug users overcome the ever-present threat of interpersonal predation and develop social connections. Closer ethnographic study by anthropologists and other drug researchers of actual drug use practices revealed that in most contexts syringe sharing was avoided and that injectors engaged in a variety of other behaviors associated with the sharing of drugs (a common behavior because users often cannot afford the cost of drugs on their own). Ethnographic studies also found that even in the absence of direct syringe sharing, the virus may be transmitted from one user to the next.

Known as "indirect sharing" (Koester and Hoffer 1994; Page 1990), these behaviors include using the syringe plunger to mix drugs, sharing drug cookers (containers like bottle caps used to dissolve drugs in water to allow injection), sharing cotton swabs (used to filter drugs to avoid needle clogging), using rinse water previously used by another person (to clean needles of potential clogs), and squirting a drug solution from one syringe into the back of another (known as backloading) to equalize the share given to each participant in a pooled drug buy. Each of these behaviors allows the contents of one syringe to make contact with the syringe of another user and potentially to transmit HIV from an infected individual to an uninfected one. Additionally, it has become clear that the sexual risk of transmission of HIV is also a significant source of infection among IDUs, as well as for non-IDUs, such as users of drugs like crack cocaine.

In our research at the Hispanic Health Council, we have sought to assess HIV risk among street IDUs like Tony. For example, besides Tony, there were 133 active IDUs recruited to participate in our Substance Abuse, Violence, and AIDS (SAVA) study. Of these, we found that the majority (69.4%) had used the Hartford Syringe Exchange Program—a harm-reduction initiative founded in 1993, following an active public health campaign led by community activists and researchers—as a source of new syringes. The syringe exchange was the most frequently mentioned source of syringes among study participants, followed by the pharmacy (42.5%) (which has been allowed since 1992 in Connecticut to sell syringes without a prescription), underground syringe sellers on the street (43.3%) (many of whom are themselves drug users and use syringe selling as a source of drug money), diabetics (33.6%) (who serve as a common supplier of new and used syringes among illicit drug users), and other sources (23.9%) (presumably a fellow drug user in most instances). As for their primary source of syringes, 46.3% reported it was the syringe exchange program and 20.1% indicated it was the pharmacy, with 14.9% saying most of their syringes came from diabetics and 11.2% saying that they bought most of their syringes from street syringe sellers.

Relatively few participants in the study reported using syringes that had previously been used by another illicit drug injector. Almost three quarters (73.1%) reported never doing so in the last 30 days and only 26% indicated that they directly shared syringes with other people. Even among these syringe sharers, the number of times they engaged in this behavior was relatively low. As a proportion of total injections, the number was even lower. Five respondents, however, indicated that they always inject with syringes previously used by others. Three of these high-risk injectors only injected a few times per month, although two were frequent injectors (namely 120 and 150 injections per month, i.e., 4–5 times a day). Further, only fourteen participants used previously used syringes for more than 10% of their injections per month. About a third of those who used syringes that had previously been used by others never used bleach to disinfect them, although over half who said they used previously used syringes told us that always cleaned them with bleach first.

In terms of indirect sharing, 63.4% of participants in the study did not share cookers or cotton filters, while 71.6% did not share syringe rinse water, and 74.6% did not share drugs mixed in someone else's syringe. Overall, we found that participants were more likely to have shared drug injection paraphernalia *other than syringes* than they were to have shared syringes. Eight of our participants said that they use syringes found on the street or in an abandoned building. One person, in fact, reported that all of his previously used syringes were "found" in such locations.

Finally, we asked participants about their use of shooting galleries—like the abandoned building where I interviewed Tony, described in chapter 1—for drug injection. A little over half of our participants (54.5%) told us that they had used a shooting gallery in the last 30 days. If they used one, moreover, they tended to do most of their injecting there. Most respondents reported, however, that they do not obtain syringes in the shooting galleries.

Looking at Tony, it is evident that he exhibits behaviors that are similar to the risk profiles of most of the other participants in this study. While he injects in shooting galleries, he gets all of his syringes from sterile syringe sources and has not shared syringes or other injection paraphernalia with others for years, with one exception. He has shared equipment in the context of a romantic relationship, much as lovers in other contexts might share a glass of wine or sips from a can of beer. This kind of exception is common among drug users, even those who are well aware of the risks. Sharing a syringe in this context—as opposed to "necessity sharing" when no other syringe is available and drug craving is intense (as sometimes happens when a drug user's only syringe breaks or clogs at the most inopportune moment)—is an act of bonding and shared fate. In the contemporary world of IDUs in the United States, especially among older, more seasoned actors on the drug scene, "relationship sharing" and "necessity sharing" are probably the two biggest direct syringe-related risks for HIV that they face.

In reviewing our SAVA data, it is evident that there is a fair degree of variability among street IDUs; their drug use and injection patterns like their personalities, appearances, or beliefs differ. In light of the fact that both the syringe exchange program and pharmacies are the only guaranteed sources of sterile syringes (Singer et al. 1997; Stopka et al. 2003), and in terms of the relatively low rates of other risk behaviors reported by participants, we concluded in this study that AIDS messages have reached and been genuinely taken up by most, but certainly not all, IDUs in Hartford. As a result, in our studies over the years we have recorded important drops in levels of HIV infection among IDUs based on the tests administered to detect HIV exposure. Tony, however, was not one of the lucky ones.

> I was first diagnosed with HIV in 1998. I had the test [in prison]. The infectious disease guy, the counselor told me. He sat me down. I started crying. Now every time I would have a cut or something, I would have to watch out. I wasn't thinking about health care, I was thinking about getting back to the [prison] dorm, I wanted to get high. And I did. I really wasn't listening to him. I was in shock. I was thinking, as soon as I get

out of here, I am going to get high. I am going to try to kill myself. I am going to be on a run [continuous use of drugs]. To be honest, I am still dealing with the shock now [seven years later]. I thought I was careful but I guess I was not careful enough. I just had a cousin in New York die of AIDS. That scared me too.

STIGMATIZATION

Despite falling rates of infection among IDUs, especially in the Northeast, AIDS has significantly affected the lives of people like Tony, not only as a life-threatening disease but also as a form of negative social labeling. As Paul Farmer and Arthur Kleinman (1989:138) argue in their paper "AIDS as Human Suffering," people living with AIDS have been subjected to "hostility and even violence [including] . . . discrimination in housing, employment, insurance, and the granting of visas." Moreover, such treatment is not simply a product of misunderstanding or lack of sympathy among those who are not afflicted. As a UNAIDS Fact Sheet on HIV/AIDS Stigma (2003) notes:

> HIV/AIDS-related stigma and discrimination play a key role in producing and reproducing relations of power and control. They cause some groups to be devalued and others to feel that they are superior. Ultimately, stigma creates and is reinforced by social inequality.

In part, AIDS stigmatization has been driven by fear. As a potentially lethal disease that appeared suddenly and quickly exacted a tremendous toll in human life and suffering, the disease has generated considerable anxiety and emotional turmoil. On the street, once a test for HIV exposure was invented, there appeared a new folk illness people referred to as "Fraids," the features of which were well expressed in the street saying: "better Fraids than AIDS" (i.e., it is better to not be tested and live with the fear that you might be infected than to be tested and learn you are dying of AIDS). Beyond this, however, AIDS was initially identified among gay men, a population that is already subject to social opprobrium and disdain in many quarters of society.

Early on, the epidemic was referred to as "the gay plague," an exclusive association that has not been easily broken by subsequent findings on the causation of HIV infection. Within a year or so of the discovery of AIDS, injection drug use was identified as another route of disease transmission. With this finding (which actually surfaced early in the epidemic but was not fully accepted because of the prevailing notion that AIDS was a disease of gay men), AIDS became firmly linked in the popular imagination with "bad behavior." From this perspective, AIDS was caused by engaging in behaviors like gay sex and illicit injection drug use that were already subject to intense moral condemnation in society at large.

From this point, it was not a far stretch to interpret AIDS as a punishment from God for sinfulness in the minds of Christian fundamentalists and others. This interpretation developed swiftly as a number of prominent conservative preachers claimed that AIDS was proof of the moral decay of America. In a television broadcast of his *The Old Time Gospel Hour*, for example, evangelist Jerry Falwell announced to his audience of believers that AIDS is "God's judgment of the homosexual promiscuity in this land" (*The Journal* 1983). As the epidemic progressed, however, and the populations suffering from AIDS began to include those who could not easily be condemned for immoral behavior (e.g., recipients of blood transfusions, babies in utero, faithful spouses of infected partners), it became clear to many religious people that viewing AIDS as punishment from God was a dangerous conclusion. The connection between immorality and AIDS was by then, however, established in the popular consciousness and continues even today to have its impact.

In our interviews with HIV-infected drug users, researchers at the Hispanic Health Council and Institute for Community Research have found quite contrasting reactions to learning of an HIV+ diagnosis. Some people experience a great sense of loss, considerable emotional distress, and tremendous fear of what awaits them. Others see their infections as a form of liberation from the weighty burden of material reality and past misbehavior, sensing an opportunity for spiritual growth. Among the latter were individuals who "spoke of a journey toward becoming a better individuals as a result of the experience of living with HIV" (Mosack et al. 2005:595).

In his own response to being HIV-infected as well as suffering from other major health problems, Tony seemed to waver between these two distant poles. At one point, he expressed a desire to become more spiritual.

> Now I got Hepatitis C, I got HIV, you know. . . . I am trying to become spiritual because I am at a crossroads in my life. . . . Where do I go from here? I was not a religious person because of my mother. She tried to force it on me. Right now it's like if I die where am I gonna go? I don't wanna die. I want to live. I never accepted God because of the things I have done in my past. And I am still doing. At the time I didn't think God or anything else could save me. Talking with people, I've realized that even if you do not believe in God, if there is something spiritual inside you, it can help you come to grips with things. I am trying to seek something spiritual. I've done a lot thinking about my past. I've killed. I've stolen. I never stole anything from my mother. But I have stolen for drugs. All my life drugs, drugs, drugs. I've done a lot of things just to get the money or the drugs.

At other points, Tony seemed to lack hope or any sense of a livable future. Yet, somehow, deep inside him, his yearning to be someone better, someone different than the person he had been all of his life, remained quietly waiting to emerge.

THE STREET DRUG SCENE

Whatever his deepest aspirations, as he faces each day Tony is caught in a pincer movement: on the one side, pressing him to use drugs is his addiction and life-long pattern of using drugs as a coping mechanism, an instant solution when hope waivers, dreaded memories loom, and the pain of public insult and private grief mount. Tony knows only too well the veracity of Shakespeare's avowal that "When sorrows come, they come not single spies, But in battalions" (Shakespeare 2005). On the other side, and as hard to escape, is the street drug scene that surrounds Tony's waking hours, with all of its illicit allures and attractions. It is a world Tony knows intimately. He has called it home for many years. As he well realizes, it is a world in continual flux; like the supermarket of legal commodities it pours old wine into new wineskins and markets them as original, seeks out novelties from far and wide and brings them to its teeming shelves, and concocts newfangled ways to combine and consume existing products.

The newest and potentially most dangerous of the "new" drugs to hit Hartford is methamphetamine, which is part of a family of semi-synthetic highly addictive pharmaceutical stimulants that have been referred to as the most "American" of drugs because they facilitate long hours of toil, enhance overall work intensity, and create a kind of frenetic industriousness—the Protestant work ethic in drug form. The twist, however, is the end result of prolonged use and the unraveling of users' lives.

Amphetamine, methamphetamine's cousin, was first synthesized from benzylmethyl acetic acid by L. Edeleano in Germany in 1887, but its stimulant properties were not fully appreciated, and the drug was largely forgotten until the late 1920s, about the time a Japanese scientist was discovering methamphetamine. Chemically, the two substances are the same, with the addition in methamphetamine of a single molecule of methyl (i.e., one atom of carbon with a set of usually three hydrogen atoms). Drug researchers—both professional and underground—know that adding methyl to a psychoactive drug alters its effects, including both the duration and potency of the high it produces because methyl increases a substance's ability to penetrate the blood/brain barrier. Moreover, the crystalline nature of methamphetamine powder makes it highly soluble in water, elevating it as a prime candidate for injection.

Users report an intense drug rush that includes prolonged feelings of euphoria, wakefulness, enhanced self-confidence, heightened strength, and aggressiveness. Reproducing these desired effects, however, requires ever-larger doses. Once the drug is metabolized by the body, withdrawal symptoms set in, including intense craving, deep melancholy, a sense of meaninglessness, extreme fatigue, lack of initiative, and gratuitous fear. Rather than an aid to diligence and hard work, in the end methamphetamine use becomes a mire of misery.

The United States is in the midst of a sweeping methamphetamine epidemic, which began in the 1980s with illicit production in underground laboratories in California and grew through wider national distribution by motorcycle and prison gangs and crime families based in Mexico as well as by the establishment of countless small labs across the country. From California and the Northwest Coast, the drug spread eastward across the Midwest during the 1990s, reaching the South and moving northward along the eastern seaboard since the turn of the 21st century.

Exemplary of the scope of the diffusion of methamphetamine, in August 2005, Operation Wildfire, a cooperative effort by the Drug Enforcement Agency and police departments in 200 cities, arrested 427 individuals involved in methamphetamine production and distribution at 56 clandestine labs, including several employees from an assisted-living facility for the elderly in Pittsburgh who were brewing the drug at work. Diffusion of the drug has resulted in endless media and government reports of significantly increased violence, damaged lives, rising medical costs, orphaned children, poisoned environments (from the toxins used in production of the drug), and painfully disrupted communities.

In our years of drug research, however, methamphetamine was not a common street drug in Hartford. There is growing evidence that this is now changing. Says Tony:

> It's in Hartford. I went to the Franklyn Theater and I got hooked up with the guy who sells it right there. I know where to get it. He's been selling it for a year now. . . . I asked this guy that I know four years ago . . . 'cause he used to sell way back, 20 years ago, and he said, "it's down Franklyn." So I went down there and I hooked up with this guy. He's a biker. I talked with him and he's got plenty too. He said it's been out a year. It's going for $50 for a gram and a half.

Deciding to purchase methamphetamine from this dealer, Tony was led to a house the dealer rented nearby, where he injected the drug, and it caused him to stay awake for the next three days.

> I just saw a lot of bikers there that's all. I didn't see no colors [gang insignia] flying. I bought a half [of a gram] so I did two shots out of that. It kept me up three days. It was clean. It was good. It wasn't like sometimes you could tell it's garbage stuff. This was clean. It was made by a pharmacist . . . somebody in school. That's what they do, they get these kids in college that are goin' into pharmacy, you know, pharmacy school and they do that, [to] make money.

The experience was disturbing despite Tony's many years of drug use.

> It was the first time I ever geeked [in this instance, he focused on visual details and was unable to move] in my life. Usually when I do cocaine I don't geek. When I mix it with dope, that stuff makes you stuck. Can't move, can't talk, you sit there, and you're just racing. Everything is going by like . . . if you were walking everything would be going by super fast. But you think you're in slow motion, you know what I mean. You can't do that too much. I'm scared of it. I couldn't do that every day. I got so geeked, looking out windows. I don't like that paranoia feeling. Cocaine never did that to me. This stuff made me geek like that. I get 10 times more high than on cocaine.

The drug induced an enhanced sensory capacity and an intense sense of fear, both for Tony and for the other people he met in the house, who, like him, had approached the dealer seeking to buy the drug.

> There were college students there too, using. They were geeking like me, I mean . . . it's crazy. Everybody looking out the windows [in fear]. It makes you panic more . . . and paranoia comes in. Even something like a door opening is scary. Your senses are like intensified . . . but you freak out, you know what I mean. You'd be like thinkin' something [was coming] underneath the door, trying to get in. You could talk as long as you got something to calm you down a little bit. I had a bundle of

dope that I sold, to the students. They didn't do that before and they're like well, they wanted to come down quicker, so they needed something to really equal [counteract the strength of the methamphetamine] and I think that's where pills [tranquilizers] come in too. Some of them use it. . . . One girl told me that she does it a little bit, you know snorts just a little bit and it helps her study. She don't do like a whole thing like she did that night but she'll do a little bit. Like, she'll buy for the whole week and she'll do a little bit, just one line and she'll start studying. It'll keep her up. They were stuck there the whole weekend. I mean geeking, that's what I mean by stuck; they were stuck.

When he finally came down, Tony decided he would never use methamphetamine again. He expressed concern, however, for what could happen to Hartford if the drug caught on with inner-city users. "It will be devastating," he feared. Given the local appeal of crack cocaine, also a stimulant, it was Tony's sense that methamphetamine could be seen as a way to solve the perennial problem of crack users: that the crack high lasts only 5–10 seconds and then another hit of the drug is needed. With methamphetamine, by contrast, a single hit would last the whole day or more.

LOVERS AND OTHER STRANGERS

In her account of intimate relationships among street drug users, from which the title of this section is taken, Waterston reports that in the corpus of drug user narratives that she analyzed the norm was "adherence to patriarchal philosophy, particularly the legitimacy of male violence and notions of sexual private property" (1993:224). If there is one way in which Tony differs from the drug users Waterston studied, it is in his attitude toward women and toward lovers in particular. He reports that he has never hit a woman, would never even consider it. Additionally, his expressed values about relationships, and his accounts of the relationships he has had, do not suggest a strongly patriarchal belief system. If anything, Tony seeks to find through a relationship, salvation from his dilemma; he is a marginalized individual, with fairly mainstream hopes and dreams that are blocked both by his own shortcomings and by structurally imposed barriers that make his most heartfelt desires difficult if not impossible to fulfill. In the end, however, his relationships with women have provided no salvation and were no less conflicted and fragile than those described by Waterston. What Tony does share with the drug users Waterston studied is a similar social location at the bottom of the American social hierarchy and an addiction to drugs, two traits that work powerfully against successful romantic relationships.

When he was younger and involved with street gangs, Tony had had numerous passing relationships, largely sexual in nature, none of which he took very seriously.

> During the gangs it was like, I wasn't tied down with just one. It was just . . . during the gang period. It was like, girls liked to hang with us. It was like, if you grabbed one by the neck, they liked that and they wanted to be with you that night. That's the way it was, you know, groupies. We called them hos . . . gang hos. They just loved to get physical. They liked rough stuff, gang bangs and all that. I never was tied down with one.

When I first met Tony, however, he had a girlfriend, Sherry, [pseudonym] who he was very serious about. She was someone with whom he hoped to leave the drug life, to establish a conventional family (which included regaining custody of her children from previous relationships), and to become the kind of person he wanted to be. He commented, "Really that's [the one real relationship] I had in my life, that lasted like six years, together on and off you know. Good times, sober . . . one year we were actually sober together." Yet, from the beginning it was clear that Tony and Sherry faced significant challenges, and fulfilling his dream would be no easy chore.

> We met when I got out of prison [the second time]. I met her through smoking rock [crack cocaine]. One thing led to another and I moved in with her. She got clean for six months and I was supposedly going to stop. I stopped smoking rock but I still had my dope habit. I stopped [using crack] 'cause she

> stopped. I figured, well, I'll give this a shot, but I wasn't going to
> give up my dope. I wasn't in love with it [crack] like I was with
> heroin. But then I started her on dope. And it's like anybody
> that truly loves dope. She loved it. Right after that she went
> back to the rock too.

The consequences for her and Tony, as well as their relationship,
were swift and severe.

> We had her kids back, then we lost everything, the kids, the
> apartment we had. I was doing good working, still getting high
> but I was working back then. Then the apartment was gone and
> the kids were taken by DCF [Department of Children and Fam-
> ilies]. She had two boys, twins, another son and a baby girl. They
> all got taken away. Me and her went to an abandoned building.

Then Sherry discovered she was pregnant, which once again
sparked hope that they could turn their lives around. Disaster
struck instead.

> She went all the way up to six months [pregnant]. But I seen
> the baby laying right there on the slab. That is the worst thing I
> have seen in my life, my child dead. The way they treated that
> child, put a towel over it and just moved it like it was garbage. I
> got mad at the hospital because of that. That was part of me
> and you're treating it like garbage. You might as well throw it
> [the garbage] in the way they were treating it. The police had
> to escort me out. They didn't arrest me . . . , but they wouldn't
> let me back to the hospital. It was like all that feeling coming
> back with God punishing me.

After spending six months living in the abandoned building,
Sherry decided to seek residential drug treatment. Soon after she
went into treatment, Tony was arrested on an old failure to appear
larceny charge stemming from a "shopping" scam and he went
back to prison for six months.

Upon his release from prison, Tony looked for Sherry and finally
found her. He had kicked his heroin habit while incarcerated and
hoped still that it might be possible to start over with her. Mean-
while, Sherry also had stopped using drugs, but she had become

involved with another man as well. When she saw that Tony was clean, she broke off her new affair and resumed her relationship with Tony. The second honeymoon was short-lived however.

> Misery loves company. Soon as we were hooked up again, bam, right back to where I was. Not the 10 or 15 bags but three or four bags. I started sniffing too and went back to the needle. So she left and moved in with her grandmother. I burned a lot of bridges. I got family, my mother is out there. But my bridges are burned; they're tired [of his drug use]. My sister is tired, mother's tired, aunts, uncles. They consider me dead right now. I borrowed money and didn't pay it back. Stupid things. Lying about what I needed the money for. Couldn't go near the house or they'd call the cops.

At this point, Tony began selling drugs again, repeating his life-long pattern.

> I was trying to sell dope too, trying to get my life back. I figured if I can start selling again I can get it back, but the progression [of addiction] was worse. . . . I always loved Sherry, you know. I just got to the point, if you can't beat 'em, join 'em. And that's . . . I think that was my big mistake with her. I don't think she loved me anymore. I think she just . . . um, she didn't respect me or anything because I gave up on her. Like I said, if you can't beat her . . . 'cause I tried . . . I tried to sell more drugs. I tried to steal more stuff. I tried to get more money so she could smoke crack, do dope and stay home. I was fightin' a losin' battle because she wanted more and more and more. Finally I just gave up and said, you know. . . . And then it got to the point [where I was asking] where's mine? You know, you're out there making money, where's mine? Where's my dope? Where's my drugs? So after a while she lost respect for me.

Soon money loomed as a constant source of tension in Tony's relationship with Sherry. She desperately wanted Tony to make more. Although she denied it, Tony felt she wanted him to make it any way possible, including dealing drugs.

> It's always money with her, money, money, money. It gets monotonous after awhile. I mean if I am working, you know, I

give her half of my money. But I need her to go out there and find a job too. I can't do it by myself. She tells me she is looking for a job and she don't. [Instead], she comes up to Hartford and hangs out. And she is arguing with me 'cause I am using the needle. She thinks that's worse than sniffing. It just makes me feel I can't do nothing right, you know what I mean? When I work, they hold back a week of my pay and when I tell her, she is gonna think I spent it. That's the way she is. She don't trust me and I trust her completely. . . . I don't understand why she won't trust me. . . . I feel our relationship is based on money not love. That's what's driving me crazy. I'm straight with her about money. If I split it with her, I split it with her.

Underlying Sherry's desire to have more money, in part, was her hope of once more getting custody of her now scattered children. At the same time, she was also caught up in her own drug dependency.

It gets to the point, I say, "Damn, you don't trust me." Then she says that she got another man that can take care of her. I said, "Go ahead, go with him. If you love him, go with him." She wants an apartment so she can get the kids back, but she wants everything the fast way. She wants it right now. I can't do that. In the past I could have but I'm not going out there to sell drugs anymore. I'm trying to find a job, a legit job. I got a legit job at night, and I'm going to school and getting paid for that every two weeks, two hundred dollars for school. I'm doing the best I can right now. With my record who is going to hire me? She keeps saying she doesn't want me to sell drugs but deep down I know she does 'cause she wants everything fast. She wants the high plus she wants the apartment. But if I do that I'm going back to jail. I am older now, I feel it in my bones. Jail would be no picnic.

In the end, Sherry left Tony. She moved to Florida with another man, only to discover that she was severely ill.

She is dying. She is in Tampa. She's got, um, . . . she's the one that gave me Hepatitis C. And right now her liver is really bad. She's on oxygen and she weighs 400 lbs. and she doesn't have that long to live. She got married and the guy is still makin' her cook dinner. Her husband gave her HIV 'cause I guess they got married and he didn't tell her that his first wife died of AIDS. But she's the only one I really did love.

The only other romantic relationship that Tony has had was with the cousin of an old gang friend of his.

And after Sherry it was just on and off flings, and I was with one other girl, Ann [pseudonym]. I was with her for a year. [Then Ann] started turning tricks [prostitution] and me being in the habit [addicted] I am trying to convince myself she's doing it for her . . . 'cause the cocaine took over her like a rocket. She needed dope in the morning, but she would smoke [crack] at night. I was never in love with her, so I convinced her she could make money hustling herself. So she used to turn tricks and what she did she did to make money. But I convinced her that I loved her and that she was doing it for both of us. I was happy as long as I had my bundle and a half a day [15 bags of heroin]. Our place was used as a crack house or to shoot up; you know, come in here to use but you got to hit me first [share the drugs]. Then I went to jail and she took off to Ohio and I haven't seen her since. They say I have a son by her. I never seen him. I don't know, but I don't have any other children to claim my own. Sherry's last kid she had, Carmen, I gave her my last name and that's my only daughter. But it's not [really] my daughter, but she has my last name. Sherry's mother has Carmen, and she won't let me see her anymore. I just gave her my last name 'cause Sherry didn't know who was the father. But I am not the father, Carmen is Black. I didn't want the baby to be, you know [a bastard] . . . so I gave her my last name.

TODAY

Despite his fear of going back to prison, when Sherry left him to go to Florida, Tony was arrested yet again for possession and sale of heroin and returned to prison for four more years. The old patterns had not changed. Yet, in significant ways Tony was not the same person, as was evident when he was released from prison in 2002. It was clear to him now that his old days as a reckless street fighter, as a go-for-broke gang member, as a smooth-talking dope dealer, as a fast-lane street drug addict, and even as a tough guy who used violence to claim respect were slipping through his fingers, travelers on the sands of time. But the hold of drugs on his body, his mind, and his will was still too strong. The following year, he was arrested again and served four months for possession. Although he managed to dodge another arrest for over a year after his release, he continued to use drugs heavily.

Then in March of 2005, after we had begun discussing writing this book, he was arrested and imprisoned for the eighth time in his life. He was caught with two bags of heroin, only enough to stave his craving for drugs for part of a day. While incarcerated, he decided to make use of his time behind bars to try and make a final break with his dependency on drugs. Despite all his setbacks and disappointments, broken dreams and dashed hopes, severe illnesses and painful memories, Tony, in Sisyphus-like fashion, began yet another effort to make a normal life for himself. At the time of this writing, he is in a residential drug treatment program, has not used drugs in six months, and has committed himself to finally living, as he puts it, "what other people call a normal life."

> I got six months clear of everything; no methadone, nothing. It feels good but I get cravings now and then. That's basically why I am getting high all the time. If I go to jail and get clean, I get out and start all over again. I still want to get high, but I can't. I really don't want to go back to jail anymore. This last three months I was in . . . oh God. Young bucks calling me "Pops." Me! "What up, Pop?" Oh man, I got to go. I got to get out of here. I never wanted to get out that bad. I used to like it in there [prison]. Not now! Too many young kids. Now I am at the recovery house. I got two more months to go there. Then I got to find a place to go after that. I am on what they call transitional support; it is a form of parole. I had no family to go to so they sent me to the recovery house. I got three months in [prison] and the rest I got to do out here at the recovery house. They have a lot of rules. You got to be in by eleven PM. I had a

couple of jobs but by the time I would get back on the bus it would be one in the morning. So I had to turn them down. There's a lot of rules. You can't talk to women. You can't do this. You can't do that. It's like being in a jail halfway house. I gotta go by what they say. I am classified as "zero tolerant." They won't take anything from me or they will call my P.O. [parole officer].

Even in this strict environment, the temptations remain, as drugs and alcohol are smuggled into the treatment center.

Three dudes got kicked out last week. One was drunk and the other two, I knew they were high. I mean, come on, I have been doing this so long. Someone told on them, they got a urine [test for substance use] and two days later they got thrown out. Yeah there's drugs in there. One guy they kicked out had like a bar in his room. They found 72 bottles of liquor.

In addition to such temptations, Tony must grapple with his own troubled emotions, those he handled for so long by self-medicating with drugs.

I keep a distance [from other patients at the recovery center] because of my anger. When I am sober, all these emotions come out and I get quick tempered. And I really don't want to do anything stupid right now. So I just keep a distance. I do what is required, and I go to my meetings [of Narcotics and Alcoholics Anonymous]. I had a part-time job, a nice job, in construction, driving a pick-up truck, but I was coming back an hour late and they wouldn't go for that. I had to get back at five and I was coming back at six. So I am not working now, I am looking.

As for his health, Tony still cannot quite face what he knows to be the truth.

To be honest, I don't even know where I am at with my health right now. I just finished medications for walking pneumonia. They saw the spots on my lung again and they want me to go back. It's the same spots from before. But I keep procrastinating. I seem to have this smoker's cough that I never had before. I have the virus [HIV] but my T-cells ain't come down yet enough to get medication. The last time I was tested was seven months ago. And with the hepatitis my enzymes are not too bad. I am supposed to see the doctor at the city clinic next week. They have a walk-in clinic. But I really don't want to find out anything right now. I am scared to find out. Right now I have HIV [but not full blown AIDS]. I think my viral load is up there, but I am scared to find out if it is enough to start the medication. That means you are on your way [toward dying]. To me it does. I wanna do it but I really don't want to find out.

Still, he tries to focus on his goals, those he has embraced for many years but has never been able to really get close to achieving. Past failures notwithstanding, Tony still can muster guarded hope for a change, a change in who he is, a change in where his life is going.

When I get out [of the recovery house], I hope to go back to that job. I will do anything in construction that he wants me to do and I will do a good job. The boss has no problem with me he said. And I have to save up enough money for an apartment once I get out. I want to live like these other so-called normal people do, which I can't seem to do. But I am going to try it. And I want to be with my girl, Norma. We've been together about eight months. Right now, she is in a halfway house, for drugs, a woman's living center. But she has been clean for a year. I had known her for a lot of years, but we just started clicking again. That's about it.

With this last comment, our last interview ended. Tony asked me if the Hispanic Health Council could help his girlfriend find housing when she gets out of treatment. We agreed that he should bring her to the council and our service staff would do their best to find her a place to live. We shook hands, and Tony walked out on to the street, craving the drugs that could so easily be acquired there but fighting that craving, trying to be enough of a tough guy—still—to defeat his drug addiction.

• Chapter 8 •

The Meaning of a Life

"One way you die like a soldier, but it's kinda like dying like a punk because you representing all the wrong things when you die in the street.

—Jose Manuel Gonzal
1977 - 1995

Engraved statement of a gang member

Street addicts are not . . . merely victims of oppressive conditions. They are also feeling and thinking human beings who are creative actors in their efforts to manage larger forces and constraints. . . . Moreover, some activities may be understood as forms of resistance although they are often highly individualistic, privatized, and self-destructive. While the feelings and thought that trigger acts of resistance have the potential to be channeled into organized political action, this has not occurred among street addicts, who are held in check by social myth and the institutionalized web within which they are caught.

—Alisse Waterston, Street Addicts in
the Political Economy

The painful symptoms of inner-city apartheid will continue to produce record numbers of substance abusers, violent criminals, and emotionally disabled and angry youth if nothing is done to reverse the trends in the United States since the later 1960s around rising relative poverty rates and escalating ethnic and class segregation.

—Philippe Bourgois, In Search of Respect

SHALIMAR THE CLOWN

After the publication of his novel *Shalimar the Clown*, noted author Salman Rushdie stated during an interview that he writes books that explore "the intersection of private lives and public affairs" and asks the questions: "To what extent are we the masters of our fate? To what extent do we make our lives, and to what extent are our lives made for us by forces beyond our control?" (Grossman 2005:6) Taking a real life rather than a fictionalized one, the intersection that is Rushdie's favored terrain as a novelist is precisely the one examined here. Perhaps it says something about our era that this intersection is of equal concern to novelist and social scientist alike. The reason for this shared concern was identified some time ago by C. Wright Mills when he noted:

> Nowadays men [sic] often feel that their private lives are a series of traps. They sense that within their everyday worlds, they cannot overcome their troubles, and in this feeling, they are often quite correct: What ordinary men are directly aware of and what they try to do are bounded by the private orbits in which they live; their visions and their powers are limited to the close-up scenes of job, family, and neighborhood; in other milieu, they remain spectators. And the more aware they become, however vaguely, of ambitions and of threats which transcend their immediate locales, the more trapped they seem to feel. (1959:3)

It remains unclear, and thus a topic of debate, just how to balance biography and social structure; there is a kind of tension in our thoughts about the relative importance of personality and the decisions of an individual versus the social worlds in which he/she is embedded from womb to tomb. Rushdie notes the role of historic events in shaping his view of this tension:

143

> I think the thing that has shifted in the modern era is that the balance of those two elements has been weighted more heavily on the side of loss of control. Our characters are no longer entirely our destinies. When those planes ran into those buildings, it didn't matter what the character of the people inside was. (Grossman 2005:6)

Of course, there is nothing that happened on 9/11 that speaks to this issue any more so than does the holocaust or the enslavement of Africans or ethnic cleansing in Eastern Europe or the horrors of Cambodia. We all know the lives of individuals can be battered about or snuffed out in an instant and not because of anything they have done or said, not because of who they are or the state of their character. People can literally be swallowed up in the events of history. And yet, some of the passengers on at least one of the planes that went down on 9/11 did not die without taking action, without attempting to assert their will on the surreal events that were taking place before their eyes and that certainly were not of their making or their choosing. Although, perhaps this too says nothing about their character either, for surely it is unlikely that the people were braver or smarter or less afraid on one of the hijacked 9/11 planes than on the others. In the end it would seem we need a dynamic model that focuses on the interplay of individual, immediate social *milieu* and socio-economic-political structure to comprehend the relationship between the lives of individuals and the historic social structures in which their lives are lived.

This is the approach taken in this book, which has explored the thoughts, feelings, and life experiences of a single individual; the social milieu of family, gang, prison, and inner-city street that have formed the primary stages of his tumultuous life drama; and the wider structure of class and other relations that have helped to construct and sustain those stages.

THE INDIVIDUAL

In these pages, I have tried to present Tony, the individual, as he is, to a large degree in his own words, warts and all, not as a romantic, inner-city street hero, but certainly not as a heartless demon, without virtue or character either. With all of his faults and moral transgressions, and his sometimes shocking tendency towards brutality and self-centered action, there is more to Tony than stereotypic pronouncements about urban street criminals, drug-crazed gangsters, and dope peddlers.

In a world of racism, where overt and hidden cruelties are inflicted on the basis of skin color or accent, somehow Tony did not embrace the vicious myth of racial superiority. Even a "low-life drug addict and dope peddler" like him knows that racism is wrong, yet many people who consider themselves to be far more virtuous than Tony ever considered himself to be seem not to understand this. Overt or covert, racism is practiced daily in our society, mostly, of course, by people who would deny they are racists. Thus we have watched the dismantling of equal opportunity practices and other civil rights gains in recent decades, resulting in growing disparities of wealth and health between Whites and people of color in this country. Nonetheless, we smugly like to view racism as something that happened in the past and is not much of a problem today.

Of course, not even Tony likes who he is, who he grew up to be. He still clings to the hope that he can be something other than he is now. In this, he does not deny his past; it haunts him and looms like a clawed fist that at any moment may reach out and pull him back. He struggles against this, hoping perhaps to find something spiritual within him, something good and untainted by his life of drug-driven criminality, something that will allow him finally to be released from his decades-long dependence on illicit chemicals so that he might find salvation.

THE SOCIAL MILIEU

What then of the role of the social milieu? There can be no doubt that Tony had a difficult early life. The confines of his world clearly were strongly shaped by his fractured family, the contrastive and conflicted parental models he saw before him, the failures of supervision, and the excitement of an outlaw street life offered by his peers. No doubt, there are others who had harsher early lives than Tony who did not succumb to drug addiction, gang membership, heinous acts of violence, the taking of lives, and the selling of dope. But, then again, Tony is hardly alone in these behaviors.

It is neither a coincidence nor some strange social concentration of poor character or immorality that explains why people who lead lives like Tony's disproportionately come from poor and working-class backgrounds and are the victims of early childhood abuse. Of course, not every boy or girl from Tony's block got swallowed up by drugs, gangs, crime, and the other sharks of the murky waters of inner-city life. Nonetheless, proportionately more did succumb compared to their peers who grew up on the tree-lined streets with their well-spaced multistory homes in the green-grass suburbs that Tony never knew (except briefly as a member of a landscaping crew cutting lawns and trimming hedges for people who neither knew nor ever thought about how lucky Tony felt just to have a job).

This is not to imply that Tony's social milieu was an empty cupboard, a list of missing items that lacked content of its own. On the contrary, like all of us, Tony grew up in and inhabited a culturally constituted world of social meanings and understandings, values, and expectations. Culture is the core concept in much of anthropology, which is not to say that anthropologists have always (or ever) agreed upon its meaning. In a classic book in the field, Clyde Kluckhohn (1949) assembled many of the primary definitions of culture, including "the total way of life of a people" and "way of thinking, feeling and believing" in a social group.

At the heart of many definitions of culture is the notion that "man is an animal suspended in webs of significance he himself has spun" (Geertz 1973:5). In other words, while we sense a material world around us with our eyes, ears, nose, hands, and other capacities, we do not live in a world of innate objects. Sunsets mean something to us, as do flowers, a meadowlark's call, or even the piercing bite of a hungry mosquito. A man with an active libido may be called a "dog," while calling a person by the name of the female counterpart of the same species, a bitch, is hurtful and angering. People are ready to die for liberty, even if it is hard to specify what precisely liberty is. They are also prepared to kill for the honor of a colored cloth if it is labeled "our flag" (or the colors of one's gang).

Cultures, all cultures, even the culture of street drug addicts, are complex and rich in symbolic content, seem natural and normal to their adherents (even when that entails hurting or even killing others, which, for one reason or another—although often differing reasons in different groups—are sanctioned in all cultures) and give meaning and purpose to life. Not only does being a drug injector require a considerable amount of cultural knowledge (such as how to acquire drugs, evaluate them, use them, and experience them, or how to survive on the street, find places to sleep, hustle money, and avoid arrest), but drug users inhabit a world that is defined by the cultures (both mainstream and street) in which they partake. Exemplary is Tony's understanding of what it means to be a man. In Tony's world, and in his own understanding, a man is tough and self-reliant. When, during the course of his life, he encounters situations in which this culturally constituted image of manliness is challenged, he sinks into confusion and self-loathing, and he struggles mightily to regain a self-image that is in tune with his cultural expectation of who he should be.

As is the case for all of us, changing a deeply ingrained, highly emotionally charged and long-held cultural understandings or associated values is no small task. But it happens. Anthropologists have come to fully appreciate culture as a dynamic, processual phenomenon rather than a fixed set of traits passed down from generation to generation. As Eric Wolf emphasizes:

> Once we locate the reality of society in historically changing, imperfectly bounded, multiple and branching alignments . . . the concept of a fixed, unitary, and bounded culture must give way to a sense of the fluidity and permeability of cultural forms. (1982:387)

Today, as a result of such rethinking, anthropologists tend to define culture as a "shifting, contested, and conflictual site of the meanings, values, norms, beliefs, traditions, and so on that make up the stuff of everyday life for some social group" (Hill-Jackson 2005:9). At the individual level, Tony struggles with aspects of both mainstream and street drug user culture, which, of course, are intertwined, rather independent systems. He is, in short, in dynamic tension with his social milieu.

THE STRUCTURE

While grasping the fundamental importance of culture is an important step in comprehending street drug life, it would be woefully incomplete if we thought of culture only in terms of learned and symbolic systems of meaning. In addition, there is the issue of structure, by which we mean the generally unequal configuration of social relations among individuals and groups within society. In other words, the issue is not simply webs of significance but how they intersect with webs of power.

Several books that carefully examine the social structures underlying the behaviors and lifeways of illicit drug using populations in the United States have appeared in recent years. In his *In Search of Respect*, Philippe Bourgois (1995) details the structural factors that shape the world of Puerto Rican youth in East Harlem, New York, leading them step by step into a life of a drug use and crack dealing. The structures in question—poverty, blocked employment opportunities, and discrimination—are real and consequential for the young men and women Bourgois lived among and studied. They are, in fact, forms of structural violence that inflict wounds no less damaging than those inflicted by the forms of physical violence they commonly provoke.

On the issue of the relationship of social milieu to structure, Bourgois argues:

> The moralistic debates that condemn deficient child-rearing practices in the inner city bemoan the absence of fathers in families [e.g., Fleisher 1995]. It is assumed that fatherlessness destroys a child's moral fiber, even though the single most overwhelming problem faced by female-headed households is poverty. (1995:287)

Notably, Tony struggled to be a father to Sherry's children. Certainly, it was his dream to be a better parent than his own father had been. But Tony could not find a way to make it work. As Bourgois further notes, "There is a clear material basis for the failure of fathers to support their progeny in stable, loving families" (1995:287). In Tony's case, his inability to find decent work and the pressures this placed on his relationship with Sherry were important factors in their inability to achieve the family life they sincerely wished for. Addiction also was a factor. But it too has roots in the social structure, as Alisse Waterston (1993), whose insightful writings are quoted in one of the epigraphs at the beginning of this chapter, shows in her book *Street Addicts in the Political Economy*.

In this volume, Waterston analyzes the U.S. political economy and the place of street drug users within it. It is her contention that an economic system that sustains an exploitable subcaste of low-cost, drug-dependent workers (who like Tony work sporadically when opportunities and life situations allow) and allows for warehousing segments of this controlled surplus labor pool in publicly funded prisons does so to curtail production costs while increasing corporate profits. Although street drug users often lack steady full-time employment, they do acquire shorter-term, blue-collar jobs of various sorts, like lawn care, door-to-door advertisement distribution, construction and repair, street clean-up and snow removal, all jobs that Tony has had at one time or another. Commonly, these jobs are located in largely unregulated, underpaid, and somewhat hidden sectors of the informal economy, and they pay no benefits.

Sociologists of work have long recognized that an effective means of lowering salaries in the working-class is the maintenance of a sector of semi-employed workers at the bottom of the labor market. This especially desperate pool of workers who are resigned to accept socially marginal, low-status (yet possibly high-risk) jobs at minimal (often subminimum) wages functions competitively to pull down the wage levels of all other groups of workers. As Waterston points out:

> As a special category, addicts are politically weak and disconnected from organized labor, thereby becoming a source of cheap, easily expendable labor. Moreover, the costs of daily reproduction are absorbed by addict-workers them-

selves. The conditions of their reproduction are quite poor
and occur at barely minimal levels. (1993:241)

Lower labor costs translate into higher profits. Moreover, when
workers from the bottom of the labor pool are not needed, they
can be easily cast off without fear of legal or labor action.

There is, in fact, nothing new in this pattern. Mintz, for example, has analyzed the role of various psychotropic drugs, including
tobacco, coffee, and tea, as cheap "drug foods" that were incorpo-
rated into popular use as low-cost food substitutes for the laboring
classes of Europe during the rise of colonialism and the subsequent rise of the capitalist mode of production. By increasing
"workers' energy output and productivity," Mintz argues, these
drugs play an important role "in balancing the accounts of capitalism" by lowering the cost of supporting a manual labor force while
increasing production (1985:148). Drugs and addicts, it appears,
do far more for society than is often recognized.

In my own study of the broader structure of changing drug use
patterns, I have sought to draw attention to illicit drug production
and distribution as a partially hidden branch of the wider capitalist
economy (Singer 2006). Dubbed "illicit drug capitalism," the $400
billion a year profit-driven global illicit drug market is far more inte-
grated with the broader economy than is often recognized. Examples of this integration include mainstream companies investing in
the illicit drug trade for quick profit, respectable banks and other
financial institutions laundering illicit drug profits, drug profits
being reinvested in legal corporations, pharmaceutical companies
boosting production to meet the illicit demand, physicians profiting
from aggressively prescribing psychotropic drugs, transportation
and delivery companies transporting illicit drugs to the market-
place, and restauranteurs and shopkeepers buying and reselling
"hot" merchandise pilfered by drug addicts from other stores.

In terms of the entwinement of these below- and aboveground
economies, money laundering is a particularly fascinating, if
deeply murky, area of economic transaction. Each year, illicit drug
corporations are able to "alchemize uncounted billions in ill-got-
ten gains into legitimate assets" (Porter 1991)—which amounts in
weight to several tons of small bills each day. A wide array of

schemes are used, and since 1989 they have been tracked and described in a monthly newsletter called the "Money Laundering Alert," which is published by Charles Intriago, who worked previously as an assistant U.S. attorney in Florida and also as counsel to a House subcommittee in Washington.

Intriago reports that offshore banks and those in other countries outside of the United States have commonly been used for laundering drug profits. For example, in 1998, 22 bank officials representing 12 different banks in Mexico were caught in a scheme to transfer "dirty" (that is, drug-connected) money to U.S. accounts and withdraw it as "clean" money to be shipped to illicit drug companies based in Mexico and Colombia. However,

> money-laundering has increasingly worked its way into Main Street, USA. In some cases, for instance, the launderers divide their money into bundles of less than $10,000—the lowest limit on cash deposits or purchases that must be reported to the IRS—and parcel them out to "Smurfs," named for those industrious little blue cartoon characters, who in turn deposit them in hundreds of banks throughout the country. With growing frequency, launderers have also been doing their washing through small businesses, such as real estate companies, car dealerships, jewelers, art galleries—anywhere they can find someone willing to sell something expensive that will hold or increase its value and who will agree to take payment in cash. (Porter 1991)

Large corporations are involved in money laundering as well. In 1995, distributors for Phillip Morris, a tobacco company, were indicted for laundering $40 million in what the government called a "black market peso" operation involving purchase of Phillip Morris products for sale in Colombia. Five years later when Phillip Morris was sued

> by a group of Colombian tax collectors who accused the company of involvement in cigarette smuggling and drug money laundering, Phillip Morris signed an agreement with Colombia pledging to prevent its products from entering the black market or being used in money laundering. (Zill and Bergman 2001)

The company, of course, did not agree to stop producing and widely distributing tobacco, the drug that takes far more lives than any of the illicit substances discussed in this book. After all, no one is going to call them a criminal, demonize them, or put them in jail for peddling tobacco.

Beyond money laundering, like other sectors of the business world, the captains of the drug industry and the illicit corporations they manage (often called cartels by the mass media) must develop mechanisms to insure the regular delivery of new or updated products, the discovery and opening of new markets, the safeguarding of existing markets from competitors and opponents, the cutting of production and distribution costs when possible, and the expansion of production and distribution. While bribery, intimidation, the flouting of legal systems, and outright violence are among the strategies used by illicit drug corporations, they are not unique to this sector of the capitalist economy, and all have been used and continue to be used by otherwise legal corporations in various times and places.

Violence has regularly been used by corporations to break workers' strikes. The Pinkerton Corporation, for example, came into being precisely for this purpose. The heads of many workers fighting for a decent wage or tolerable working conditions have been cracked open by company thugs, the police, and even the military in attacks no less vicious than those Tony has participated in or witnessed. Private corporate armies, in fact, are now common and active around the world; quite literally, war itself has become a commodity produced and sold by corporations for a profit (P. Singer 2003). Another expression of the use of violence by legal corporations is the mobilization of paramilitary forces to gain access to oil or mineral resources. In the Republic of Sudan, for example, large stretches of oil-rich land have been cleared of their inhabitants by vicious attacks by paramilitary forces (and subsequently advertised as "uninhabited" land) and then drilled by major oil corporations (Christian AID 2001).

Other forms of illicit behavior by legal corporations are also common. To cite but one example from an endless list of similar or far more disturbing instances of such behavior by respected corporations, in 2005 two very wealthy Hartford-based insurance companies, either of which could have been Tony's sister's employer, were named in a $30 million settlement of a law suit filed by Connecticut's attorney general alleging that the companies had entered into secret pacts with insurance agents to steer small business customers to them without informing customers this was happening (Levick 2005). Since independent insurance agents are supposed to be helping their customers buy the right insurance for them at the best price, sordid payback schemes of this sort are illegal under fair trade and insurance practice laws, and the insurance companies know it. To facilitate the back-door agreement, customers steered to the insurance companies were handled by employees who were instructed to lie to callers and tell them that they represented the insurance agent when they in fact were employees of the insurance companies.

Prosecutors believe such schemes are a national epidemic, part and parcel of a regular and broad pattern of profit-enhancing, control-avoiding white-collar crime by major corporations. Each year, the major financial magazines publish special issues about the sales levels, assets, profits, and market shares of the world's largest corporations. The point of these reports is to identify and glowingly honor the biggest and most profitable corporations. So glorified have corporations and their executives become that there is even a street gang in Los Angeles known as the Businessmen.

In response to what he feels are often hidden chapters in corporate success stories, reporter Russell Mokhiber publishes the online *Corporate Crime Reporter*, which identifies the top corporate criminals. Noted Mokhiber (1999), "Nine out the 30 companies that comprise the Dow Jones Industrial Index are convicted corporate criminals." Commonly, however, media reporting and legal prosecution of corporate crime is downplayed. Sometimes the courts aid in this effort by supersealing cases brought against corporations. In September 2003, for example, Essex County, New Jersey, Superior Court Judge Theodore Winard sealed a court decision that blocked news organizations from having access to documents and proceedings in a fraud suit brought by several former employees against a major

References

Asbury, Herbert
1928   *The Gangs of New York*. Garden City, NJ: Alfred Knopf.

Baer, Hans, Merrill Singer, and Ida Susser
2003   *Medical Anthropology and the World System: A Critical Perspective*. 2nd edition. Westport, CT: Bergin and Garvey.

Bebow, J.
2004   Flood of Heroin Ravaging City. *Chicago Tribune*, January 30, p. 1.

Bogardus, Emory
1926   *The City Boy and His Problems: A Survey of Boy Life in Los Angeles*. Los Angeles: Rotary Club.

Booth, Martin
1996   *Opium: A History*. New York: St. Martin's Griffin.

Bourdieu, Pierre
1990   *In Other Words: Essays Towards a Reflexive Sociology*. Cambridge: Polity.

Bourgois, Philippe
1995   *In Search of Respect: Selling Crack in El Barrio*. Cambridge: Cambridge University Press.

Bourroughs, William
1953   *Junkie*. New York: Ace Books.

Brook, David, Judith Brook, Linda Richter, Martin Whiteman, Orlando Arencibia-Mireles, and Joseph Masci
2002   Marijuana Use Among the Adolescent Children of High-Risk Drug-Abusing Fathers. *The American Journal on Addictions* 11:95–110.

Brook, Judith, Martin Whiteman, Ann Scovell Gordon, and David Brook
1984   Identification with Parental Attributes and its Relationship to Son's
         Personality and Drug Use. *Developmental Psychology* 20:1111–1119.

Brook, David, Judith Brook, Elizabeth Rubenstone, Chensu Zhang, Merrill
Singer, and Michael Duke
2003   Alcohol Use in Adolescents Whose Fathers Abuse Drugs. *Journal of Addictive Diseases* 22(1):11–34.

Brodwin, Paul
1996   *Medicine and Morality in Haiti: The Contest for Healing Power.*
         Cambridge: Cambridge University Press.

Brown, Claude
1965   *Manchild in the Promised Land.* New York: Penguin Books.

Bureau of Justice Statistics
2005   Statistics on Drugs and Crime. Available online: www.ojp.usdoj.
         gov/bjs/drugs.htm (accessed September 20, 2005).

CDC (Centers for Disease Control and Prevention)
2002   *HIV/AIDS Surveillance Report: Cases of HIV Infection and AIDS in
         the United States, 2002.* Vol. 14. Available online: www.cdc.gov/
         hiv/stats/hasr1402.htm (accessed September 20, 2005).
2003   *HIV/AIDS Surveillance Report: Cases of HIV Infection and AIDS in the
         United States, 2003.* Vol. 15. Available online: www.cdc.gov/hiv/
         stats/20035/SurveillanceReport.htm (accessed September 20, 2005).

Chien, Arnold, Margaret Connors, and Kenneth Fox
2000   The Drug War in Perspective. In *Dying for Growth: Global Inequality and the Health of the Poor.* Jim Yong Kim, Joyce Millen,
         Alec Irwin, and John Gershman, Eds. Pp. 293–330. Monroe,
         ME: Common Courage Press.

Christian AID
2001   *The Scorched Earth: Oil, War and Corruption.* London: Christian
         AID.

Cintron, Ralph
1997   *Angel's Town: Chero Ways, Gang Life, and Rhetorics of the Everyday.* Boston, Beacon Press.

Chopp, Rebecca
1986   *The Praxis of Suffering.* Maryknoll, NY: Orbis.

Cleaver, Eldrige
1968   *Soul On Ice.* New York: Delta Publishing.

Cloward, Richard and Lloyd Ohlin
1960   *Delinquency and Opportunity.* New York: Free Press.

Coffin, Phillip
2000   Preventing Heroin Overdose: Pragmatic Approaches. Available online: www.lindesmith.org/library/ODconferenceaudio.html

Compton, M.
1994   Cold-Pressor Pain Tolerance in Opiate and Cocaine Abusers: Correlates of Drug Type and Use Status. *Journal of Pain and Symptom Management* 9(7):462–473.

Compton, P., V. Charuvastra, K. Kintaudi, and W. Ling
2000   Pain Responses in Methadone-Maintained Opioid Abusers. *Journal of Pain and Symptom Management* 20(4):237–245.

Copeland, L., J. Budd, J. Robertson, and R. Elton
2004   Changing Patterns in Causes of Death in a Cohort of Injecting Drug Users, 1980–2001. *Archives of Internal Medicine* 164(11):1214–1220.

Courtwright, David, Herman Joseph, and Don Des Jarlais
1989   *Addicts Who Survived: An Oral History of Narcotic Use in America, 1923–1965.* Knoxville: University of Tennessee Press.

Curtis, Ric and Ansley Hamid
1999   Neighborhood Violence in New York and Indigenous Attempts to Contain It: The Mediating Role of the Third Crown of the Latin Kings. In *Integrating Cultural, Observational and Epidemiological Approaches in the Prevention of Drug Abuse and HIV/AIDS.* Patricia Marshall, Merrill Singer, and Michael Clatts, Eds. Pp. 143–171. Washington, DC: The National Institute on Drug Abuse.

Darke, S., D. Ross, D. Zador, and S. Sunjic
2000   Heroin-Related Deaths in New South Wales, Australia, 1992–1996. *Drug and Alcohol Dependence* 60, 141–150.

Davidson, R. Theodore
1978   Chicano Prisoners: The Key to San Quentin. In *Urban Anthropology in the United States: Four Cases.* George and Louise Spindler, Eds. Pp. 7–118. New York: Holt, Rhinehart and Winston.

De Quincey, Thomas
1822   *Confessions of an English Opium Eater.* New York: F. M. Lupton Publishing Co.

Decker, Scott and Barrik VanWinkle.
1996   *Life in the Gang: Family, Friends, and Violence.* New York: Cambridge University Press.

Dewalt, B. and Perti Pelto
1985   *Micro and Macro Levels of Analysis in Anthropology.* Boulder, CO: Westview Press.

English, T. J.
1990   *The Westies: The Irish Mob.* New York: G. P. Putnam's Sons.
2005   *Paddy Whacked: The Untold Story of the Irish American Gangster.* New York: Regan Books.

Fabelo, Tony and Lisa Riechers
1990   *Drug Use and Recidivism of Texas Prisoners.* Austin, TX: Criminal Justice Policy Council.

Farmer, Paul and Arthur Kleinman
1989   AIDS as Human Suffering. *Dædalus* 118(2):135–160.

Feucht, Thomas and Andrew Keyser
1999   Reducing Drug Use in Prison: The Pennsylvania Approach. *National Institute of Justice Journal*, October:11–15.

Fleisher, Mark
1995   *Beggars & Thieves: Lives of Urban Street Criminals.* Madison: The University of Wisconsin Press.

Gamella, Juan
1994   The Spread of Intravenous Drug Use and AIDS in a Neighborhood in Spain. *Medical Anthropology Quarterly* 8(2):131–160.

Gans, Herbert
1962   *The Urban Villagers.* New York: The Free Press.

Garcia-Hallcom, Francine
2000   Inaccurate Definitions Exaggerate the Gang Threat. In *Opposing Viewpoints: Gangs,* Laura K. Egendorf, Ed. San Diego: Greenhaven Press.

Geertz, Clifford
1973   *The Interpretation of Cultures.* New York: Basic Books.

Goffman, Erving
1961   *Asylums. Essays on the Social Situation of Mental patients and Other Inmates.* New York: Doubleday Anchor.

Goode, E.
1984   *Drugs in American Society.* New York: Alfred A. Knopf.

Grossman, Lev
2005   10 Questions for Salman Rushdie. *Time* 166(9): 6.

Hagedorn, John
1994a "Homeboys, Dope Fiends, Legits, and New Jacks." *Criminology* 32:197–217.
1994b "Neighborhoods, Markets, and Gang Drug Organization." *Journal of Research in Crime and Delinquency* 31:264–294.

Harper, Janice
2002 *Endangered Species: Health, Illness and Death among Madagascar's People of the Forest.* Durham, NC: Carolina Academic Press.

Hechler, David
2004 Behind Closed Doors. The National Law Journal, January 12. Available online: www.law.com/jsp/nlj/PubArticleNLJ.jsp?id= 1073667908602.

Hill, Karl, James Howell, J. David Hawkins, and Sara Battin-Pearson
1999 Childhood Risk Factors for Adolescent Gang Membership: Results from the Seattle Development Project. *Journal of Research in Crime and Delinquency* 36(3): 300–322.

Hill-Jackson, Valerie
2005 Culture Matters in High Risk, Lead Poisoned Communities. *Practicing Anthropology* 27(3): 9–14.

Hills, Stuart
1980 *Demystifying Social Deviance.* New York: McGraw-Hill Book Company.

Hughes, Patrick
1977 *Behind the Wall of Respect.* Chicago: University of Chicago Press.

Hunt, L. and C. Chambers
1976 *Heroin Epidemics: A Study of Heroin Use in the United States, 1965–1975.* New York: Spectrum.

Inciardi, James
1986 *The War on Drugs: Heroin, Cocaine, Crime, and Public Policy.* Mountain View, CA: Mayfield Publishing Co.

Kane, Stephanie and C. Dotson
1997 HIV Risk and Injecting Drug Use: Implications for Rural Jails. *Crime and Delinquency* 43(2):169–185.

Kane, Stephanie and Theresa Mason
2001 AIDS and Criminal Justice. In *Annual Review of Anthropology*, Vol. 30. William Durham, Ed. Pp. 457–480. Palo Alto, CA: Annual Reviews.

Keiser, R. Lincoln
1969   *The Vice Lords: Warriors of the Streets*. New York: Holt, Rhinehart and Winston.

Khantzian, E.
1985   The Self-Medication Hypothesis of Addictive Disorders: Focus on Heroin and Cocaine Dependence. *American Journal of Psychiatry* 142:1259–1264.

Khantzian, E., J. Mack, and A. Schatzberg
1974   Heroin Use as an Attempt to Cope: Clinical Observation. *American Journal of Psychiatry* 131:160–164.

Kleinman, Arthur, Veena Das, and Margaret Lock, Eds.
1997   *Social Suffering*. Berkeley: University of California Press.

Kluckhohn, Clyde
1949   *Mirror for Man*. New York: Whittlesey.

Koester, Stephen and Lee Hoffer
1994   "Indirect Sharing": Additional HIV Risks Associated with Drug Injection. *AIDS and Public Policy Journal* 2:100–104.

Levick, Diane
2005   Insurance Broker Settles Suit for $30 Million. *The Hartford Courant*, September 1, pp. 1 and 14.

McCall, Michael and Judith Wittner
1990   The Good News About Life History. In *Symbolic Interaction and Cultural Studies*, Howard Becker and Michael McCall, Eds. Pp. 4–89. Chicago: University of Chicago Press.

Miller, Walter
1958   Lower Class Culture as a Generating Milieu of Gang Delinquency. *Journal of Social Issues* 14:5–19.

Mills, C. Wright
1959   *The Sociological Imagination*. Oxford: Oxford University Press.

Mokhiber, Robert
1999   Top 100 Corporate Criminals of the Decade. *The Corporate Crime Reporter*. Available online: www.corporatecrimereporter.com/top100.html (accessed September 20, 2005).

Meyer, David R.
1976   *Urban Change in Central Connecticut: From Farm to Factory to Urban Pastoralism*. Cambridge: Cambridge University Press.

Milberger, S., S. Faraone, J. Biederman, M. Chu, and J. Feighner
1999   Substance Use Disorders in High-Risk Adolescent Offspring. *American Journal on Addiction* 8:211–219.

Mintz, Sidney
1974   *Worker in the Cane: A Puerto Rican Life History.* New York: W. W. Norton.
1985   *Sweetness and Power.* New York: Penguin Books.

Moore, Joan
1978   *Homeboys—Gangs, Drugs, and Prison in the Barrios of Los Angeles.* Philadelphia: Temple University Press.
1990   Mexican-American Women Addicts: The Influence of Family Background. In *Drugs in Hispanic Communities.* Ronald Glick and Joan Moore, Eds. Pp. 127–154. New Brunswick, NJ: Rutgers University Press.
1993   Gangs, Drugs and Violence. In *Gangs—The Origin and Impact of Youth Gangs in the United States*, Scott Cummings and Daniel Monti, Eds. Pp. 27–47. New York: The State University of New York Press.

Mosack, Katie, Mary Ann Abbott, Merrill Singer, Margaret Weeks, and Lucy Rohena
2005   If I Didn't Have HIV I'd Be Dead Now: Illness Narratives of Drug Users Living with HIV/AIDS. *Qualitative Health Research* 15(5):586–605.

National Institute of Justice
2000   *Arrestee Drug Abuse Monitoring* (ADAM). Washington, DC: Government Printing Office.

Neale, J.
2000   Suicidal Intent in Non-fatal Illicit Drug Overdose. *Addiction* 95(1):85–93.

NIDA
1999   *Principles of Drug Addiction Treatment: A Research-based Guide.* Washington, DC: National Institute on Drug Abuse.

Padilla, Felix
1992   *The Gang as an American Enterprise.* New Brunswick, NJ: Rutgers University Press.

Padilla, Felix and Lourdes Santiago
1993   *Outside the Wall: A Puerto Rican Woman's Struggle.* New Brunswick, NJ: Rutgers University Press.

Page, J. Bryan
1990   Shooting Scenarios and Risk of HIV Infection. *American Behavioral Scientist* 33(4):478–490.
2004   Drug Use. In *Encyclopedia of Medical Anthropology*, Carol Ember and Melvin Ember, Eds. Pp. 374–382. New York: Klouwer Academic/Plenum Publishers.

Pepper, Art and Laurie Pepper
1999   *Straight Life*. New York: Da Capo Press.

Pearlin, L. and C. Radabaugh
1976   Economic Strains and the Coping Functions of Alcohol. *American Journal of Sociology* 82:652–663.

Porter, Bruce
1991   Where to Get Some (Drug) Money. Available online: www.archives.cjr.org/year/91/5/drug_laundering.asp

Rettig, Richard P.
1977   *Manny: A Criminal Addict's Story*. Long Grove, IL: Waveland Press (1999).

Riis, Jacob
1892   *The Children of the Poor*. New York: Arne Press.

Romero-Daza, Nancy, Margaret Weeks, and Merrill Singer.
1998/   Much More Than HIV! The Reality of Life on the Streets for
1999   Drug-Using Sex Workers in Inner City Hartford. *International Quarterly of Community Health Education* 18(1):107–119.
2003   "Nobody Gives a Damn if I Live or Die": Violence, Drugs and Street-Level Prostitution in Inner-City Hartford. *Medical Anthropology* 22: 233–259.

Rubin, Lillian
1976   *Worlds of Pain: Life in the Working-Class Family*. New York: Basic Books.

Rubin, Theodore
1961   *In the Life*. New York: Macmillan.

Sands, Bill
1965   *My Shadow Ran Fast*. Englewood Cliffs, NJ: Prentice-Hall.

Sapp-Grant, Isis (as told to Rosemarie Robotham)
2000   A Need for Power and Respect Encourages Gang Behavior. In *Opposing Viewpoints: Gangs*. Laura K. Egendorf, Ed. San Diego: Greenhaven Press.

Scheper-Hughes, Nancy and Margaret Lock
1986   Speaking "Truth" to Illness: Metaphors, Reification, and a Pedagogy for Patients. *Medical Anthropology Quarterly* 17:137–140.

Schneider, Eric
1999   *Vampires, Dragons, and Egyptian Gangs: Youth Gangs in Postwar New York.* Princeton: Princeton University Press.

Schwarcz, Vera
1997   The Pane of Sorrow: Public Uses of Personal Grief in Modern China. In *Social Suffering.* Arthur Kleinman, Veena Das, and Margaret Lock, Eds. Pp. 119–148. Berkeley: University of California Press.

Shakespeare, William
2005   *Hamlet* 4.5.78–79. *The Complete Works of William Shakespeare.* Available online: http://www-tech.mit.edu/shakespeare/ (accessed September 2, 2005).

Shaw, Clifford
1976   *The Natural History of a Delinquent Career.* Chicago: University of Chicago Press.

Singer, Merrill
1985   Family Comes First: An Examination of the Social Networks of Skid Row Men. *Human Organization* 44(2):137–142.
1996   A Dose of Drugs, A Touch of Violence, A Case of AIDS: Conceptualizing the SAVA Syndemic. *Free Inquiry in Creative Sociology* 24(2):99–110.
1997   Articulating Personal Experience and Political Economy in the AIDS Epidemic: The Case of Carlos Torres. In *The Political Economy of AIDS,* Merrill Singer, Ed. Pp. 61–74. Amityville, NY: Baywood Publishing.
2002   From to Illegality to Terrorism: A Dangerous New Wrinkle in the Demonization of Drug Users. *Newsletter of the Society of Applied Anthropology* 13(2):3–4.
2006   *Something Dangerous: Emergent and Changing Illicit Drug Use and Community Health.* Long Grove, IL: Waveland Press.

Singer, Merrill and Roberto Garcia
1989   Becoming A Puerto Rican Espiritista: Life History of a Female Healer. In *Women as Healers,* Carol Shepherd McClain, Ed. Pp. 157–185. New Brunswick, NJ: Rutgers University Press.

Singer, Merrill, David Himmelgreen, Margaret Weeks, Kim Radda, and Rolando Martinez
1997   Changing the Environment of AIDS Risk: Findings on Syringe Exchange and Pharmacy Sale of Syringes in Hartford, CT. *Medical Anthropology* 18(1):107–130.

Singer, Merrill and Greg Mirhej
2004   The Understudied Supply Side: Public Policy Implications of the Illicit Drug Trade in Hartford, CT. *Harvard Health Policy Review* 5(2):36–47.

Singer, Merrill, Glenn Scott, Scott Wilson, Delia Easton, and Margaret Weeks
2001   "War Stories": AIDS Prevention and the Street Narratives of Drug Users. *Quarterly Health Review* 11(5):589–611.

Singer, Merrill, Freddie Valentín, Hans Baer, and Zhongke Jia
1992   Why Does Juan Garcia Have a Drinking Problem?: The Perspective of Critical Medical Anthropology. *Medical Anthropology* 14(1):77–108.

Singer, P.
2003   *Corporate Warriors: The Rise of the Privatized Military Industrial Complex.* Ithaca, NY: Cornell University Press.

Spergel, Irving
1995   *The Youth Gang Problem.* New York: Oxford University Press.

Spergel, Irving and G. David Curry
1993   The National Youth Gang Survey: A Research and Development Process. In *The Gang Intervention Handbook*, A. Goldstein and C. R. Huff, Eds. Pp. 359–400. Champaign, IL: Research Press.

Sporer, Karl A.
1999   Acute Heroin Overdose. *Annals of Internal Medicine* 130(7):584–590.

Spradley, James
1970   *You Owe Yourself a Drunk.* Prospect Heights, IL: Waveland Press (2000).

Stopka, Thomas, Merrill Singer, Claudia Santelices, and Julie Eiserman
2003   Public Health Interventionists, Penny Capitalists, or Sources of Risk? Assessing Street Syringe Sellers in Hartford, Connecticut. *Substance Use & Misuse* 38(9):1339–1370.

Sutherland, Edwin
1937   *Professional Thief.* Chicago: University of Chicago Press.

Tavares, Hermano, Monica L. Zilberman, David C. Hodgins, and Nady el-Guebaly
2005   Comparison of Craving between Pathological Gamblers and Alcoholics. *Alcoholism: Clinical & Experimental Research*. 29(8):1427–1431.

The Journal
1983   Broadcast on AIDS (July 6, 1983). CBS TV.

The Sentencing Project
2005   New Incarceration Figures: Growth in Population Continues. Available online: www.sentencingproject.org/pdfs/1044.pdf (accessed September 20, 2005).

Thomas, Piri
1967   *Down These Mean Streets*. New York: Knopf.

Thrasher, Frederick
1927   *The Gang*. Chicago: University of Chicago Press.

UNAIDS
2002   *World AIDS Campaign 2002–2003: HIV/AIDS-related Stigma and Discrimination*. Geneva: Joint United Nations Program on HIV/AIDS.

U.S. Sentencing Commission
2004   Recidivism and the "First Offender." Washington, DC: U.S. Sentencing Commission.

Vigil, James Diego
2002   *A Rainbow of Gangs: Street Cultures in the Mega-City*. Austin: University of Texas Press.

Vuckovic, Nancy
1999   Fast Relief: Buying Time with Medications. *Medical Anthropology Quarterly* 13(1):15–68.

Waldorf, Dan
1973   *Careers in Dope*. Englewood Cliffs, NJ: Prentice-Hall.

Wallace, Anthony
1970   *Culture and Personality*. 2nd Edition. New York: Random House.

Waterston, Alisse
1993   *Street Addicts in the Political Economy*. Philadelphia: Temple University Press.

Wolf, Eric
1982   *Europe and the People without History.* Berkeley: University of California Press.

X, Malcolm
1965   *The Autobiography of Malcolm X.* New York: Grove Press.

Yablonsky, Lewis
1962   *The Violent Gang.* Baltimore: Penguin.
2000   Poor Parenting Causes Some Children to Join Gangs. In *Opposing Viewpoints: Gangs.* Laura K. Egendorf, Ed. San Diego: Greenhaven Press.

Yang, C.
2001   Holding the Line in Heroin City. ABC News.Com. March 21, 2001. (http://abcnews.go.com/sections/us/DailyNews/heroin010314_cops.html).

Zill, Oriana and Lowell Bergman
2001   U.S. Business and Money Laundering. PBS Frontline. Available online: www.pbs.org/wgbh/pages/frontline/shows/drugs/special/us.html

Index